ON HIGH POTENCIES AND HOMŒOPATHICS.

CLINICAL CASES AND OBSERVATIONS,

BY

B. FINCKE, M. D.,

OF BROOKLYN, N. Y.

WITH

AN APPENDIX,

Containing Hahnemann's Original Views and Rules on the Homoeopathic Dose, Chronologically Arranged.

Natura nullibi magis quam in minimis tota.—Plinius.

PHILADELPHIA:

PUBLISHED BY A. J. TAFEL, HOMŒOPATHIC PHARMACY,

No. 48 North Ninth Street.

1865.

King & Baird, Printers, 607 Sansom Street, Philadelphia.

CLINICAL CASES AND OBSERVATIONS.

FIRST SERIES.

Man kann sie fast nicht zu klein geben.
HAHNEMANN (*Chron. Krankh.*, 2nd. ED., 1835, I., p. 149.)

THE following report presents a selection from a series of cases in which I administered High Dilution Potencies* with success.

The Potencies employed in these cases were Dilutions made after the centesimal scale, and were prepared by myself about 1850; some from Triturations, some from Tinctura fortis, some with succussion by means of a strong steel-spring, and some with a single jerk of the hand.

The prescription is quantitatively denoted by a fraction, the numerator being the number of the globules used (about the size of mustard seed), and the denominator giving the exact number of the successive centigrade dilutions, including the triturations or tinctura fortis respectively.

The nosological designations of the cases are intended merely as a convenience for registration.

CASES.

1. STRANGURIA.—Mr. D., of Frankfort on M., Germany, fifty years old, tailor, short and stout, choleric, cured by me of a liver complaint within the last year; took the last medicine for it in June, 1851.

---

* For particulars, as to history and various kinds of Potencies, see the article on "Homœopathic Notation," in the Proceedings of the Seventh Annual Meeting of the American Institute of Homœopathy, 1860, p. 117; and in the American Homœopathic Review, Vol. II. p. 451.

On September 31st, 1851, he complained of frequent desire to urinate, with severe pains, during which lumps of blood passed with difficulty through the urethral canal, and pressure after urinating. *Nux vom.* $\frac{2}{100}$. The urine passed after that clear and without difficulty.

2. PLEURODYNIA TRAUMATICA.—C. G., of Frankfort on M., Germany, sixteen years old, apprentice, small stature, dark-blonde, active, (with inherited gout).

October, 1851. Complained of stinging pain at a spot in the right side of his chest, precisely where he was stabbed some years ago. The pain impaired his respiration. *Arnica m.* $\frac{2}{1100}$. After that the pain occurred twice during the next week and never after.

3. ARTHRITIS CHRONICA PEDUM.—The same lad, after the experience just reported, November 29th, 1851, asked for medicine for his gout inherited from his father. The pain was in his feet and exceedingly severe, so that he could hardly bear anything on the affected parts. *Sulphur* $\frac{2}{1000}$. Immediately after taking this dose, patient felt a stitch going from the right shoulder-blade toward the middle of the back; this pain increased and went down into both knees. Stinging in the knee-joint, particularly when walking; sometimes the legs got stiff; slow walking in a moderately warm room was pleasant, but brisk walking aggravated. All this occurred the first day after taking the medicine.

December 11th, 1856. Met patient on the South ferry-boat, to Brooklyn, N. Y.; he stated, that since the above occurrence he had suffered no more from gout, nor had the stitch in his side returned. His general appearance had changed very much in his favor.

4. TUSSIS SPASMODICA.—Lottchen L., a girl of Frankfort on M., Germany, six years old, small in stature, lively and delicate, treated by an eminent allœopathic physician for six months for a dry, spasmodic, exhausting cough, and without

success. November 28th, 1851, *Bellad.* $\frac{1}{1400}$. Cured in a few days.

5. TUSSIS SPASMODICA.—George L., eight years old, brother of the above patient, was treated allœopathically without effect for a similar long standing, dry, wheezing, spasmodic cough, which affected his chest very much. November 28th, 1851. *Bell.* $\frac{1}{360}$. This one dose cured him in a few days.

6. DYSMENORRHŒA.—Miss Sophia H., of Frankfort on M., Germany, twenty-five years old, dark complexion, small stature, active, but somewhat inclined to depression of spirits, complained of cramps in the abdomen and violent pains in her back previous to menstruating, so that she was compelled to lie down. January 29th, 1852. *Puls.* $\frac{2}{5000}$. Prompt relief and no return of pains.

7. ANGINA FAUCIUM.—Friedrich H., of Frankfort on M., Germany, seventeen years old, apprentice, of dark complexion, tall, scrofulous, had burning in his throat and a sensation as if it were swollen, exciting a dry cough in the morning. March 13th, 1852. *Sulph.* $\frac{2}{20000}$. Cured promptly.

8. HÆMORRHOIDES CŒCÆ.—N. of Brunswick, Germany, forty years old, emigrant passenger on board the *Jason*, bound to New York, a sturdy fellow of dark complexion, complained of blind hæmorrhoids; itching and burning in the anus; distention of the abdomen and constipation. He had moreover sea-sickness and vomited everything he took. Sallow countenance. July 20th, 1852. *Nux vom.* $\frac{3}{100}$.

July 21st. Improvement about the anus; stool; abdomen soft. Soon after all his complaints disappeared, and did not come on during the remaining three weeks of the voyage.

9. OPHTHALMIA RHEUMATICA.—Mrs. B., of German descent, fifty-two years old, of rheumatic diathesis; caught cold, had stinging pains in the eyes; inflammation of the

bulbous and palpebral conjunctiva; could not bear the light and her sight had diminished. April 3rd, 1852. *Sulph.* $\frac{2}{200000}$. Got well next day.

10. CORNEITIS.—Johanna F., ten months old, of German descent, scrofulous, presented a milk-white spot as large as a millet-seed on the cornea, the whole conjunctiva and part of the cornea being inflamed; tongue coated white; urinating in the night difficult, with crying. August 15th, 1852. *Sulph.* $\frac{1}{200000}$. In a few days all the symptoms disappeared.

11. DIARRHŒA INFANTILIS.—N., a boy of one year and a half old, has a watery diarrhœa with colic. January, 1854. *Cham.* v. $\frac{1}{1730}$. Recovered promptly.

12. CHOLERA INFANTUM.—Thomas H., of Irish descent, six months old, had convulsions two months ago, and has suffered from vomiting and purging, aggravated a great deal the last eleven days.

August 29th, 1854. In very hot and dry weather, the patient was found extremely emaciated, with a face like an old man, hands and feet cold; incessant vomiting of greenish-yellow water and of the milk taken, as he is nursing all the time; watery diarrhœa; penetrating cries, with convulsive movements of hands and feet; sleep with half open eyes; boring of the head into the pillow and carrying of the hand to the back of the head; abdomen hard; no teeth yet. *Verat. a.* $\frac{1}{2400}$ to the child; *Verat. a.* $\frac{2}{12}$ to the mother, to be taken in a tumbler half full of water, one tea-spoonful every three hours.

August 31st. The child was reported recovered. Patient had no attack of sickness until the following summer, when a very slight touch of the summer complaint was easily overcome.

13. PHTHISIS PULMONALIS.—Mrs. Congetta M., thirty-four years old, a lady of Italian extraction, native of Tunis, in

Africa, lived in the East until about two years ago, when she came to this country; was enfeebled by many troubles, physical and mental: mother of seven children, the youngest of whom is one year old; of dark complexion and sanguino-nervous temperament; speaks seven languages.

January 17th, 1855. Complained of a hollow hard cough hurting her chest and head, with a pressing forward of the eyes; and thick yellowish purulent expectoration, excited by burning pains in the pit of the throat, which continued during the coughing. Dullness under the right clavicle; mucous rattle in the right upper lung anteriorly, in expiration and inspiration; puerile respiration in the left upper lung; pains under the sternum when sewing; great emaciation; sallow countenance; hollow sunken eyes with dark rings around; irregular chills. There was a small mole over the left brow.

Patient suffered habitually from copious and prolonged menstruation, which, however, she stated was not considered a disorder in the East. In former pregnancies she had submitted to the custom, there prevailing, of bleeding from the arm. Those of her children who were born in the East are frequently affected with epistaxis. One of her boys, thirteen years old, who has been under my observation for the last six years, is a Hæmophile and usually enjoys good health under continued homœopathic treatment. *Phos.* $\frac{2}{5000}$.

January 24th. Patient much improved; she still coughed hard, especially in cold weather. *Phos.* $\frac{2}{5000}$. After that all the symptoms disappeared.

14. RHEUMATISMUS PEDUM.—Mr. N., of German descent, forty years old, a full-sized gentleman, blonde, of rheumatic diathesis, complained of weakness in his ankle-joints; sudden bending of the ankles, and swelling around them while walking. February 13th, 1856. *Carb. an.* $\frac{3}{1000}$. Immediately after taking the medicine, patient felt light and comfortable. The next day the weakness and swelling disappeared.

15. ANASARCA.—The same gentleman complained on a

hot summer evening, 1856, of swelling, dryness, tension, and heaviness all over and through his whole body; of burning of the feet and want of energy, so that he was obliged to lie down. *Bryonia* $\frac{2}{9000}$ relieved him instantaneously and permanently.

16. GASTROSIS.—Mr. S. of German descent, married, forty-five years old, vender of vegetables, of dark complexion, middle size, coffee-drinker, had attacks of vomiting ever since his eighteenth year. He used a great deal of purgatives for it, and some time ago a white powder, which was followed by the most horrible vomiting, convulsions, contraction of the feet, and cold perspiration. After that he left off every kind of medicine. Patient had a good appetite; liked his food well peppered and salted; had a constant bitter taste in his mouth: felt nauseated all the time, and vomited immediately whatever he ate. Moreover, he threw up bitter water all day, and in the night, when it woke him up; rumbling in the bowels; tongue pale, slightly coated; taking pork made him perfectly woe-begone; yellow countenance; emaciation. March 8th, 1856. *Nux vom.* $\frac{4}{5000}$.

December 1st, 1858. Patient got well directly, and has been growing stout ever since.

17. DIARRHŒA INFANTILIS.—N., an infant, was affected for some time with a greenish diarrhœa, which lately changed to brownish, slimy discharges. July 7th, 1856. *China* $\frac{1}{8000}$ in a tumbler half full of water, one tea-spoonful every three hours. Before one-half of this solution was taken, the child was well.

18. HEMICRANIA MERCURIALIS.—Mrs. Sarah A., a widow, forty-five years old, probably of Irish extraction, slender and small in stature, dark complexion, nervous temperament, patient of the Brooklyn Hom. Dispensary; suffered from excruciating stinging pain all over the left side of her head, including the region of the left eye and ear, commencing at

five P.M., and increasing during the night to the extreme. Gums spongy and dark red; teeth almost all decayed from the abuse of mercury; trembling all over; extreme sensitiveness. *Bell.*3, *Bell.*6, *Nux v.*6, *Ver.*6, *Ars.*1, from June 17th to July 15th, had been given without the desired effect.

August 1st, 1856. Patient was entirely given up to despair, and used latterly large doses of Asafœtida in order to kill the pain, also without effect. *Merc. v.* $\frac{2}{3000}$.

August 4th. Patient reported, that she had been relieved of the pain immediately, and that she had come to report it, and thought she did not need any more medicine.

19. FEBRIS GASTRICA.—Ellen, an Irish cook, about twenty-five years old, dark complexion, good-natured, complained, after hard working and lifting, of soreness in and tenderness of the epigastrium; nausea; disagreeable taste; pressure in the forehead, worse in stooping; want of appetite; tongue furred and coated yellow; fever; small, quick, and frequent pulse; dry, hot skin; flushed face; great weakness. She suffered usually in the morning from cramp in the stomach. August 27th, 1856. *Nux vom.* $\frac{2}{5000}$; after some aggravation patient got well next day.

20. ABSCESSUS PROCESSUS MASTOIDEI.—Ernest D., a boy of German descent, eight years old, two years ago put a bean into his right ear. It was taken out with severe pain and some injection made into the ear. Since that time stinking matter has been discharged from the ear every now and then. His hearing was not impaired. A few days before seeing him, an abscess formed behind the right ear, covering the mastoid process, causing the most excruciating pain, preventing rest and sleep; fluctuating slightly; face sallow and disfigured; entire want of appetite for some time. After warm chamomile poultice, highly offensive matter ran out of the ear, but the pains continued unabated.

August 8th, 1856, 4 P.M. Directed the poultice to be taken off and gave him some pellets *Hep. s. c.* 1750 to be taken in a tumbler half full of water, one tea-spoonful every three hours.

After the first dose the patient felt immediate relief. The abscess opened the same night during sleep, and healed without further trouble.

21. TUSSIS STOMACHICA.—Mary M., of German descent, two and a half years old, blonde, played with a kitten four or five months previous to my seeing her. Since then she coughed every night, with effort to vomit and was wasting away gradually. An allœopathic physician, supposing that some of the kitten's hair had got into her stomach, relieved her somewhat by purgatives for a few nights, but then the complaint returned every night, so that she could not sleep. Eating sugar and drinking water ameliorated; stools frequent, of pale clayey color, three or four times a day; she had whooping cough when nine months old. November 22d, 1856. *Sulph.* $\frac{1}{20000}$.

November 29th. The very night after taking the medicine, the cough subsided, and the child has slept well ever since.

22. RETENTIO URINÆ.—Martin K., of Irish descent, sixteen months old, had retention of urine from twelve o'clock A.M. to two P.M., with great tenderness of abdomen, and then passage of some hot dark-colored urine, staining the clothes; no urine passed since; top of the head very hot, with beating of the pulse in the fontanel, which was not entirely closed; cold perspiration; screaming wildly. Before the retention, urine was passed profusely; rather inclined to costiveness. The mother has piles and liver complaint and was nursing the patient. July 1st, 1857. *Nux vom.* $\frac{1}{5000}$ to the baby; *Nux vom.* $\frac{2}{5000}$ to the mother.

July 31st. Patient has been well since he took the medicine.

23. CHOLERA NOSTRAS.—Mr. S., mason by trade, forty-two years old, single, of German descent, intemperate, tall, lean, dark blonde, stammering, had worked hard in Gowanus,

during the heat in July, 1857, and had drunk much bad water there.

July 19th. He lost his appetite entirely, loathing foul meat at his meal.

July 25th. Patient presented himself in a pitiable condition; very much debilitated; face of earthen hue; tongue thickly coated yellow, with bitter taste; moderate thirst; throwing up whatever he drinks, sometimes immediately after taking it; at the same time, yellowish watery diarrhœa; severe cramps in the calves during the passage, and pains around the navel after it; pulse slow and hard, not very full. *Verat a.* $\frac{6}{2400}$ in a tumbler half full of water, one tea-spoonful every two hours. He rallied very soon, and has been well since.

24. STRANGURIA.—Miss N., an American lady, thirteen years old, of unusual embonpoint, suffered for many years past from difficulties in urinating, and was under homœopathic treatment.

In September, 1857, she complained of painful urging to pass urine, followed by not more than one drop of dark-colored urine at a time under the most excruciating pain. *Canth.* $\frac{2}{1630}$ in a tumbler half full of water, one tea-spoonful every two hours. After the first dose the difficulty disappeared.

25. INTERMITTENS.—Mr. H., clerk, twenty-six years of age, of German descent, dark blonde, phlegmatic, had been affected with a cold in his head for a week. Two nights before seeing me, he noticed a disagreeable taste in his mouth; dry lips; flatulency, and nausea. The next morning, pressing heaviness over the eyes, much aggravated on moving the eyeballs, on making a step, and at the least noise. He took some gin, which rose up continually from his stomach; took only a cup of chocolate for dinner. About five, P.M., shaking chill, as if his body were suspended in the air and shaken, with clattering of his teeth; cold hands

and coldness of the skin for one hour. After a few pellets of *Aconite*$_{30}$ in some water, which he took for himself, the shaking left, but the chilliness continued. No sleep; terrible heat; pains in the back, moving from the sacrum upward to the region between the shoulders; aching over the eyes; toward midnight, perspiration with griping in the bowels; then one or two hours of sleep. At three, A.M., awoke with head-ache, which was ameliorated by laying the head higher; his bowels had been moved the day before; pains along the lower part of his back as far as the shoulder-blades. This forenoon, while writing, a stitch along the back which drew him crookedly together, with an involuntary loud cry; now and then chills; pulse small, quick, 96; pressing heaviness upon the eyeballs on moving them; no appetite; no thirst; periodical nausea; dry tickling cough. December 15, 1857. *Puls.* $\frac{4}{5000}$.

December 16th. When he got home from the office, he slept very well until three or four, A.M., next morning. On waking, he found himself in a profuse perspiration, which lasted until seven or half-past, A. M. The head-ache was less severe and went to the vertex, and thence to the occiput and to the nape of the neck. The griping in the abdomen was of a spasmodic character, and occurred every ten minutes; better after passing wind. Constipation; felt tolerably well all day until five, P.M., when he got a chill lasting ten minutes, but less severe than the last one, with pain in the vertex and in the nape of the neck, higher up than before. The patient slept well and woke up at five, A.M., next morning in perspiration, but otherwise comfortable; no appetite; pulse small and soft; weakness; head-ache gone and returning only after continued writing; rising of wind with running water in the mouth; hands sometimes warm, sometimes cold, and in the latter case the nails turn blue. *Sacch. lat.*, three powders, one every night. The patient had no further attack, and felt stronger than ever before.

26. HERNIA INGUINALIS INCARCERATA.—Charles C., of

German descent, nineteen months old, was brought to the office from New York, June 6th, 1858, three, P.M., with the following symptoms:—Since morning, short laborious breathing; inclination to vomit; stool in the morning green, probably from vegetables he took the day before; left inguinal hernia as large as his fist, bluish-red, hard and extremely sensitive to the touch when lying down, better when sitting up. Every attempt to reduce it by taxis was out of the question. Frequent, almost uncountable pulse; hot hands; continual gasping. *Acon.* $\frac{10}{1100}$.

Shortly, after the patient was carried away in the arms of his mother, he fell asleep, and when he got home it was found that the hernia had receded.

27. INTERMITTENS.—Mrs. R., an Irish washer-woman, about forty years old, got wet on the upper part of her body, and since then has had chills every day after dinner, followed by heat in the evening; night before seeing me, perspiration after the heat, all without thirst. Much dull pain in the head, especially in the forehead, across the chest and in the arms; stiffness of the neck; pulse weak; tongue torn, red; looks most miserable. September 19th, 1858, nine, A.M. *Puls.* $\frac{6}{5000}$.

After some dizziness in the head next day, she got well without another paroxysm.

28. INTERMITTENS.—Mrs. N., an American lady, thirty years old, dark blonde, mother of six children, did not feel quite well for some days last week, being up at night with the baby several times. While sitting in church this forenoon, she got an internal chill all over, though the skin was warm to the touch; with nausea; thirst; ghastly face; throbbing in her head, on the top and in her temples; and red eyes, lasting until half-past two, P.M., when it passed into a heat with less redness of the eyes, continued headache, and bloatedness of the face. Patient had an old rheumatic pain for two weeks in the lower back and on the

top of the right hip, which returned the night before last, and last night, and a very little this morning. Tongue coarse; bowels regular; nurses a baby eight months old; but has not much milk; had fever and ague when a child, and was then treated with large doses of Peruvian bark. February 13th, 1859. *Nat. mur.* $\frac{2}{350}$ after the paroxysm in the evening.

February 14th, four, P.M. The chill passed off; headache lasted until this morning. Patient could not sleep on account of feeling as if bruised all over, weak and tired.

February 15th. Patient felt quite well; she remained so without another chill.

29. SCIRRHUS MAMMÆ.—Mrs. B., a woman of Swiss descent thirty-seven years old, three weeks married, thin, of dark complexion; had been always regularly menstruated until her voyage from Europe to this country, when her catamenia got out of order, but was regular for three months previous to consulting me. While on board the ship, she drank Chamomile tea instead of coffee. She had several years ago an abscess at the left hip-joint. Her teeth almost all decayed. In the fall of 1858, a hard lump gradually grew, accompanied by severe darting pains, on the upper part of her sternum, attaining in ten or twelve days the size of a hen's egg; it then decreased under the application of warm poultices and of a yellow ointment, getting softer and softer until it disappeared.

April 4th, 1859. Patient had suffered for a fortnight from a swelling of her right mamma. It presents a stone-hard lump, extending from the left half of her right mamma to the median line of the sternum, overlapping the normal boundary as large as her fist. Since the 3rd instant, the lower part of the sternum projected considerably as if the bone were swollen. Small hard tumor of hazel-nut size in the arm-pit. Severe darting pains in the right side of the chest, all over the right mamma and in the swelling at the breast-bone, lancinating as far as the arm-pit and along the right side of the chest toward the back. These pains prevent sleep, as they become insufferable when in bed. Although she had a good appetite, patient appeared ill-fed and thin. Some red blotches on the upper part of the chest anteriorly. She could not lie down otherwise than on her back, nor turn from that position on account of the pains. Used flax-seed poultice, which did not ease the pain nor help anything. *Carb. an.* $\frac{2}{1000}$.

April 28th, 1859. During the first three days after giving the medicine, the pains were aggravated and then decreased gradually; only now and then a darting pain was felt in the hard places. The lumps were less hard and nothing of the tumor under the axilla was left. No more medicine given.

March 6th, 1860. Patient is very well; was delivered of a vigorous boy a fortnight ago, and her mammary apparatus is in the best condition. Lumps and pains had by the end of May gradually, and wholly, disappeared.

30. CEPHALALGIA AB ABLACTATIONE.—Mrs. N., twenty years old; dark complexion, phlegmatic, complained of heavy acute pain across the forehead over the eyes, worse in stooping; the eyes were quite red when she rose up again. Patient was weaning a baby, and has a superabundance of milk flowing away involuntarily. Depression of spirits; very slight leucorrhea; was very hot the previous night and took *Acon.*$_3$ for it, which moderated the heat, but not the head-ache. October 23d, 1859. *Puls.* $\frac{3}{7000}$.

October 25th. One hour after taking the medicine the head-ache was gone, the milk dried up without further inconvenience, and she recovered.

31. DENTITIO DIFFICILIS.—Sophia S., of German descent, two years old, with light blonde hair and blue eyes, complained for some time of her legs. The last molar tooth was just cutting through with its first point. In the afternoon, effort to vomit and choking; towards evening, apparently itching in the arms; in the night, delirium, talking during

sleep, pointing with the finger to the forehead, better by laying the hand on it; floccilegium; much heat, alternately in head and hands; sometimes large round red spots on both cheeks; much thirst; watery discharge from her nose; watering of the eyes, which look pale and have a staring expression; dry cough. January 9th, 1860. *Bell.* $\frac{1}{6000}$ in Sacch. lactis.

February 3d. Patient got well immediately after taking this dose.

32. DISTORTIO CARPI.—Mrs. N., thirty years old, of German descent, full habit, sprained her left wrist last August on lifting by her left hand a heavy bowl of peaches over the table. Since then, she has suffered when using the hand with shooting pains in the wrist, as in inflammatory rheumatism, very much aggravated at night in bed. Patient used Opodeldoc liniment at the time of the accident, to no avail. The pains had been more severe for the last few days and nights. There was a slight swelling upon the middle of the left wrist, and want of strength in the part. March 29th, 1860. *Rhus tox.* $\frac{2}{10000}$.

April 7th. Patient had no pain the next night after the medicine, but the following day all along, severe jumping, shooting, stinging, flashing, hot pains, such as are observed in inflammatory rheumatism, not only in the affected spot which appeared slightly swollen, but all around and through the whole wrist, and almost as far as the elbow. Toward night the pains subsided. Since then the wrist has been wholly free from pain and swelling, and as strong as ever.

OBSERVATIONS.

Cum sæpe a minimis maxima proficiscantur.

LEIBNITZ.

In conclusion I beg to submit the following observations:

1. The action and efficaciousness of homœopathic remedies are not limited to the lower preparations, nor to the thirtieth, or 200th Potency, but their healing properties are preserved, propagated, and exalted through

a series of still higher Potencies, being evident even in the 20,000th centigrade Dilution of Sulphur.

2. The question, where the terminus of the medical action and efficaciousness of homœopathic remedies is to be found at all by potentiation, is still open.

3. High Potencies prove efficacious and curative in single doses.

4. High Potencies sometimes present the phenomenon of homœopathic aggravation.

5. High Potencies prepared by dilution with a single jerk of the hand, prove efficacious and curative.

6. High Potencies prepared by dilution with a strong succussion, sometimes do not present any homœopathic aggravation.

7. Higher potentiation seems to be the means of rendering the remedy assimilable and thus homœopathically active.

8. The curative action and effect of homœopathic remedies, as already foreseen by Hahnemann (*Organon*, fifth edition, § 275), is in every individual case conditionated and governed by the dose as well as by the homœopathicity of the drug.

9. The curative action and effect of High Potencies being established as a fact, *any* Potency, and consequently *any High* Potency, may be *the* dose in any given case.

10. From this arises a necessity, to individualize the dose as well as the remedy.

11. The chances of individualizing the dose increase in the ratio, in which, by experience, a greater variety of Potencies is placed under our command.

12. In this view the posological problem grows in importance, and, as it can only be conquered by "pure experiments, careful observation, and correct experience," (*Organon*, § 278,) it is of the greatest moment to multiply the experiments with higher Potencies.

13. Such experiments should be made with the experimenters' own preparations, and on the human organism, which so far, and especially in its diseased condition, appears to be the only reagent, or test, delicate enough for substances as fine as such medicines.

14. Homœopathic Potencies, that is to say, those fine preparations of medicaments which are effected by the peculiar method and operation of Hahnemann's invention, are, in fact, and strictly speaking, not mere divisions only of the drug into its parts, but are rather differentiations and progressions, being at the same time, as it were, successive reproductions and propagations of the medical properties of the drug and its given part.

15. For the required calculations, a mere arithmetical enumeration of the particles into which Potentiation is assumed to divide the given quantity of the drug, is insufficient and dubious, being apt to cause mistake and confusion, as it has done already; and being unwieldly, too, on

account of the immense array of its figures; and, in fact, not adequately corresponding to the real truth in the matter.

16. For a theory of Potentiation, the labors of Korsakoff and Joslin are pre-eminently valuable.

17. For the practice with High Potencies, by experience so far, the rule holds good: **THE MORE SUSCEPTIBLE THE ORGANISM, THE HIGHER THE POTENCY AND THE FINER THE DOSE.**

18. For a scientific explanation of the curative action and efficiency of High Potencies, it might serve, to apply to Therapia a certain Law of Nature, which was discovered and mathematically established by Maupertuis. This is the *Law of the Least Quantity of Action*, by some called LEX PARSIMONIAE, or Law of Thrift; ridiculed by Voltaire, defended and explained by Euler, happily touched upon by Franklin, and developed by Lagrange. It is thus enunciated by the discoverer:—"*La quantitè d'action necessaire pour causer quelque changement dans la nature, est la plus petite qu'il soit possible,*"—i. e., the quantity of action necessary to effect any change in nature is the least possible; and again: "*Lorsqu'il arrive un changement dans la Nature, la quantitè d'action necessaire pour le changement est la plus petite qu'il soit possible,*"—*i. e.*, when a change occurs in nature, the quantity of action necessary for the change is the least possible.—(*Oeuv. Dresde*, 1752, p. 41.)*

19 According to this general principle, the decisive moment is always a Minimum, an Infinitesimal. Apply this to our Therapeutics, and it will be perceived, that the least possible dose is the highest potency and necessarily sufficient to turn the scale, that is, to effect the cure—always provided the remedy being homœopathically correct.

20. This *Law of the Least Action* (MAXIMA MINIMIS) appears to be an essential and necessary complement of the *Law of Homœopathicity* (SIMILIA SIMILIBUS), and co-ordinate with it.

---

* Professor PEIRCE says, "This great proposition which was announced by its illustrious author with the seriousness and reverence of a true philosopher, is the more remarkable, that, derived from purely metaphysical doctrines, and taken in combination with the Law of Power, which likewise reposes directly upon a metaphysical basis, it leads at once to the usual form of the dynamical equations."—(*Analytical Mechanics*, Boston, 1855, p. 416.)

CLINICAL CASES AND OBSERVATIONS.

SECOND SERIES.

The possibility of communicating medical properties to an indifferent body without the medium of a liquid, without trituration, without commixtion, nay, without material division, is a fact new in Homœopathy, and highly important for theory and practice.

KORSAKOFF, 1831.

My first report on High Potencies contains cases of treatment with High Dilution Potencies.

The following presents a series of cases in which I administered High Potencies of another and different kind and preparation. They were made in the dry way, about 1850, and in this manner: I took one or more globules of the thirtieth centesimal Dilution Potency (medicated in the ratio of Gtt. i. . Gr. X.), put them into a ʒ ii vial, containing about 2,000 unmedicated globules (70 to Gr. i.), and shook them moderately, and in every direction, some by means of a little sand-mill constructed for the purpose, some by the hand only, long enough to have every globule brought in contact with the others.

This mode of preparing Potencies, it will be perceived, is similar to Korsakoff's medicating globules without Dilution, but it differs from Korsakoff's method in the ratio of medication, and in the mode of succussion, also probably in the size of the globules. Korsakoff medicated 1,000 globules with one globule of the fifteen hundreth centigrade Dilution of Sulphur with manual succussion for one minute, and 13,500 globules with one globule of the thirtieth centigrade Dilution of Sulphur with manual succussion for five minutes. Hahnemann, at the time, approved of this method of Korsakoff's in emphatic terms.

In order to distinguish this kind of Potencies from the Dilution and other Potencies, I propose for them the name of *Contact Potencies* and a Notation by the sign ($_c$) with the Potency number above ($\frac{1}{c}$,) where the fractional figure gives the number of globules of a centesimal Dilution Potency, from which the Contact Potency ($_c$) is made. Thus, *Puls.* $\frac{2}{30}$ $\frac{1}{c}$, means two globules of the first (bimillesimal) Contact Potency from the thirtieth centesimal Dilution Potency out of one drop of the tinctura fortis of Pulsatilla.

CASES.

1. LACTATIO NIMIA.—Mrs. C., of Frankfort on Main, Germany, dark complexioned, small stature, mother of ten children, the youngest of whom is nursing yet.

July 30th, 1851. Presents the following symptoms; general weakness, from prolonged lactation especially in the back; violent pressing-out pains in the forehead, as if the eyes would fall out, especially at night; scalp painful to the touch; yellowish face; on taking a full breath, the breath seems to remain suspended in the chest, with long stitches through the middle of the chest, as far as the back; appetite good; abdomen meteoristic and painful to the touch; violent diarrhœa; heaviness of the legs; chilliness of the whole body, especially in the back; restless sleep and frightful dreams; talking during sleep; irritability, vexatiousness; great prostration. Patient has menstruated for some time past, and had suffered on several previous occasions in her life from considerable loss of blood. *China* $\frac{2}{30}$ $\frac{1}{c}$.

A few hours after the medicine, the menses made their appearance, three days too soon, and as copious as a hemorrhage of the womb, of normal blood, lasting for six days, when the patient felt better.

July 9th. Nine days after taking the medicine, the dyspnœa increased to such a degree that it was feared her breath would stop entirely; when in such agony she would take hold of anything she could reach with her hands. The breathing was very deep and accompanied with long stitches through her chest into her back.

July 14th (fourteen days after taking the medicine). The asthmatic attacks are renewed. The child was weaned eight days after taking the medicine without any difficulty about the breast. *Bry.* $\frac{2}{30}$ $\frac{1}{c}$.

July 15th. The patient had lost her appetite, which, however, soon returned. Breathing was laborious and deep, accompanied with short stitches proceeding from the interior of the right side of the chest as far as the left shoulder.

July 16th, at midnight, exactly twenty-four hours after taking the last medicine, the patient had headache, and noticed a sudden appearance of milk in the mamma which was already dried up; at the same time felt drawing in one of her calves, as if from fatigue. After that she rallied in a short time.

2. OTALGIA.—O. N., American girl of German descent, aged seven years, blonde hair, blue eyes, very lively.

March 29th, 1857.—In the forenoon felt violent pains in her right ear, probably caused by exposure to draught of air. Her father had given her *Bell.* $\frac{1}{30}$.

One, P. M. The pains continue unchanged and seem to be worse, because she is now screaming, which is quite unusual with her when suffering pain. *Cham.* $\frac{1}{30}$. This dose first aggravated still more, and then brought some relief, but the pains soon returned. *Cham. v.* $\frac{1}{30}$ $\frac{1}{c}$ did nothing. About two, p. m., *Puls.* $\frac{12}{30}$ $\frac{1}{c}$. After that the pains were aggravated again, and the patient rolled about on the sofa, crying aloud. I then advised her to sit up. She did so, and a few moments after the pains subsided permanently, proving beyond doubt that this was the effect of the Pulsatilla (cf. Hahnemann's Reine Arzneimittellehre, 3d edition, Vol. II., Sympt. 646 and Note).

3. CROUP.—N., American girl, fourteen months old, scro fulous, dark-complexioned.

March 27th, 1857.—After a catarrhal stadium which lasted two days, during a dry, harsh and cold wind, started from her sleep, at about eleven, p. m., with a sudden violent coughing-spell, resembling precisely the barking of a hoarse dog; there was high fever, drowsiness, dread to cough, putting the forefinger into the mouth, hard and short breathing, restlessness. After *Spong. t.* $\frac{4}{30}$, she became quiet for some time, though the hard and short breathing continued. In about half an hour she coughed again. Some catarrhal sound was now mixed with the croupy one. *Spong. t.* $\frac{1}{30}$. After that she was somewhat relieved, and fell into a doze. Twenty minutes later she had another and more severe attack. The breathing was short, hard and loud; she pushed the head backwards; eyes half shut, face red with a bluish tint, involuntary motion of the left hand and of the feet, throwing herself on her mother's bosom for help. She then had a slighter cough than before, which, however, was more harassing and threatened to suffocate her. I now gave her some globules of *Spong. t.* $\frac{1}{30}$ $\frac{1}{c}$, prepared in the afternoon of that day. After this dose she became easier, and having repeated the dose twenty minutes later, I left the little patient sleeping quietly on her mother's lap. Next morning the cough was loose. The croup disappeared, and did not come on again.

4. COLICA.—Miss N., an American lady, a sensitive invalid, twenty-six years old, of fine cerebral development, suffering for years from a spinal disease, resulting from external injury.

March, 1857. Complains of colic. A medical friend of her's had given her several remedies without effect. After the administration of one dose of *Nux vom.* $\frac{2}{30}$ $\frac{1}{c}$, the colic yielded readily without producing the homœopathic aggravation of Nux vom., which with her is invariably brought on when given in lower Potencies, even as high as 100 (centes.), viz., constant disagreeable urging to urinate, with frequent and copious micturition, and prostration. From the following, it appears that even the six-hundredth centesimal Dilution of *Arsen. a.* was too low to prevent serious aggravation, which, however, subsided promptly after the use of *Nux vom.* 5,000.

September 20th, 1857. Prescribed for scorbutic affection of the mouth, throat and stomach, of a high degree, *Ars.* $\frac{1}{600}$, to be dissolved in one gill of water, and only one teaspoonful to be taken.

September 21st, TEN, A. M. Fifteen minutes after taking the first dose, the patient began to pass watery urine every ten or fifteen minutes, and in consequence a pain, which she describes as bearing resemblance to a toothache, came on in a place of the coccygeal region, where she was hurt; at the same time bearing down in the genital region. *Nux vom.* $\frac{1}{5000}$. The urinary difficulty ceased immediately, and the patient was relieved of her other complaints.

5. STOMATITIS.—The same patient.

April 11th, 1857. Complains of cankers at the root and left side of her tongue, which presented deeply-excavated sores of pea-size, covered with a whitish secretion. These were removed within two days by the use of *Ars.* $\frac{3}{30}$ $\frac{1}{c}$, every three hours.

6. CROUP.—C. N., three and a half years old, American boy, of German descent, dark blonde, hazel eyes, good-natured, of fine nervous organization.

January 14th, 1858, at 10.30, P. M. Awoke suddenly with a rough, deep, hollow, barking cough. *Spong. t.* 30, 1100, 1500. Some globules of each of these Potencies dissolved in one gill of water, one teaspoonful to be taken after every coughing spell. The cough did not moderate, but the patient began to perspire about the throat and chest. Hoarseness came on gradually and increased until 11.30, p. m., when the cough presented a hoarse, stifled sound, in addition to the deep metallic barking tone. The inspiration was laborious, with a whistling noise, and the speech was broken from the impending hoarseness; at the same time, cheeks red and hot, forehead cool, hands hot, pulse not accelerated, perspiration. *Bell.* 30 $\frac{1}{c}$ relieved the hoarseness in half an hour, and diminished the cough, which assumed again the hollow metallic barking sound, but was less frequent. After another dose of *Bell.* 6 $\frac{1}{c}$, profuse perspiration broke out; the patient yawned much and sneezed three times.

January 15th, at 12.30, A. M. I left him quietly sleeping. The croup was gone.

7. COFFEISMUS.—Mrs. D., of Frankfort on Main, Germany, thirty-two years old, blonde, blue eyes, was in the habit of sitting much and drinking strong coffee.

October 27th, 1850. Reported violent headache with peevishness and vexatiousness, want of sleep, short dry cough, and nervousness in general. *Nux vom.* $\frac{2}{30}$ $\frac{1}{c}$. After that, all the symptoms subsided.

8. INCONTINENTIA URINÆ NOCT.—Charles M., American, of German descent, two and three-quarter years old.

October 14th, 1856. Wet his bed for the last two nights, somewhat loose in his bowels, looks thin, sometimes dark around the eyes, no worms observed. *Cina* $\frac{1}{30}$ $\frac{1}{c}$. Wet his bed no more.

9. DYSENTERIA.—Mrs. N., fifty-two years old, of English descent, tall and stout, with dark hair and blue eyes, and a syphilitic taint in her system, caught cold whilst perspiring and was taken with dysentery March 27th, 1857. The following symptoms were reported:

March 31st, 1857. Awful pains in her bowels and across her back, like labor-pains; incessant straining and slight bloody discharges every half hour. Starch was taken several times without avail. The patient had the cholera in the summer, six years ago. *Nux vom.* $\frac{6}{3000}$, to be taken in one gill of water, one teaspoonful every two hours.

April 2d. Discharges once an hour, containing less blood, more white, flesh-like, inodorous substance, and streaks of bright blood with tenesmus; incessant straining without effect; tenderness of the abdomen; grumbling in the bowels; dreadful pains across the bowels and in the back, like labor-pains; urine scanty, very hot and red, with sediment; pain in the head, "as if it would come apart;" pale face. *Colch. aut.* $\frac{1}{30}$ $\frac{1}{c}$, prepared on the spot, three globules to be taken dry after every passage.

April 3d, 1857. The patient took one dose once an hour, and in her own words reported: "After I had taken nine pills, it stopped the pain wonderfully." She had, yesterday, a discharge every one or two hours; none in the night, which was passed in sound sleep; two bright yellow fæcal discharges this morning, with bearing-down pain in the bowels, the last one less severe; urine normal. *Colch. aut.*, as above, to be continued.

April 4th, 1857. Patient had, yesterday, about eight yellow fæcal discharges. This morning only two. The last one consisted of white flesh-like substance with a streak of blood and pale yellow matter without odor; five minutes before the passage, pain in the bowels; slept all night; face natural; some cramp in the sole of the right foot for five minutes, a symptom which she never had before. *Colch. aut.*, as above, to be continued, three globules after every discharge.

April 11th, 1857. Patient had now and then some pain in her bowels, which subsided after taking the globules. Bowels regular now. Had, last evening, giddiness, pain in the back of her head, and a kind of a rheumatic pain in her back, between the hinges, as she had two months ago when passing red gravel. All these symptoms disappeared in the morning. She took the globules twice a day until yesterday morning, when she took the last. Feels very weak yet. Appetite poor. *China* $\frac{2}{30}$ $\frac{1}{c}$, two powders, one to be taken every night, dry. After that she recovered.

OBSERVATIONS.

Even the smallest quantities become important when they get large co-efficients.
HERBART.

In conclusion, I beg to submit the following observations:

1. High Contact Potencies prove efficacious and curative in single doses.

2. They sometimes present the phenomenon of homœopathic aggravation.

3. They have not the aggravation which follows the use of lower and higher Dilution Potencies—in the fourth case above reported.

4. They exert their action immediately, as well as ten years after preparation.

5. The potentiating by Contact is a mode of refining homœopathic remedies by which a degree of fineness is attained different from that by Dilution.

6. Succussion does not seem to constitute an essential element in the preparation of High Contact Potencies.

7. Practically, the action of High Contact Potencies presents the peculiar distinctness of the action of High Potencies in general, and operates specifically to the point, clearly reflecting the pathogenetic characteristics of the homœopathic remedy, precisely covering the individual and most important symptoms, and promptly removing the same.

8. Their action, by this specificness of character, avoids wasting any of the elements of the organism and drawing any more on the same than is exactly required for the restoration of health.

9. They are great economizers of life and health, operating in subserviency to the general Laws of Nature, which always accomplishes the greatest good with the least expenditure of force.

10. Consequently, High Contact Potencies are most valuable and available for the purpose of meeting peculiar and special shades of susceptibility in the organism, which the close observer perceives in the given case by strict individualization.

11. Pharmacologically, Potentiation by dry Contact proves to be another mode of propagating and successively improving, reproducing, and proportionally exalting the medical properties of homœopathic drugs.

12. On this basis, whatever mathematical calculations may be required, they will have to be not mere arithmetical multiplications, or divisions, or formations of powers; but calculations of proportions and progressions, involving the Law of the Series and the higher branches of Analysis, whilst for the present it is sufficient for all practical purposes, to have the Potencies numbered, that is, counted as often as the process of Potentiation by dry Contact took place successively.

13. Scientifically, Potentiation by dry Contact appears to be effected by

a bare bringing together of unmedicated globules with medicated ones, without an intervening medium; the only medium apparent being the air:—*Action in presence.*

14. Therefore, it may properly, with Korsakoff and Hahnemann, be regarded as similar or equivalent to medicating the globules by infection or contagion.

15. In this view, an analogy, if not more, is presented with the action of hypothetic poison, or nosopœsis of miasmatic and contagious character, which acts, as it were, as High Contact Potency of matter prepared in Nature's own laboratory.

16. The fact being established, that medical properties are communicated by mere dry Contact, or Action in Presence, there is no reason, why we should not assume, that the organism can be medicated in like manner: —*Homœopathization.*

17. If so, this would give a satisfactory explanation of the fact, that Homœopathic High Potencies do communicate their medical properties, upon application to the organism by mere Contact, and exert their remedial or curative action upon it directly, sometimes instantaneously, and independently of digestion and circulation.

18. Such decided affection of the organism through a High Contact Potency is not more wonderful, than the analogical fact, that a bar of polished metal, being indifferent in a horizontal position, becomes electrical merely by being placed vertically, as has recently been shown by Henry.

19. Here may be well applied, what Draper states in relation to Allotropism: "Does not all this show, that substances may be, as it were, in a quiescent state, and on the application of what may perhaps seem the most insignificant cause, may suddenly assume activity and forthwith satisfy their chemical affinities?"

20. Since mere Contact of so refined a substance as a Homœopathic High Potency, is certainly an infinitesimal, or least possible quantity of action, clearly this medication by Contact, as well as, indeed, every homœopathic cure, is quantitatively governed, conditionated, and explained, by the universal principle of Maupertuis, before alluded to.

21. On this principle, the least possible quantity of action being sufficient to cause a change, the curative properties and action of the homœopathic remedy are actually and necessarily regulated and governed by its preparation and application; in other words: *the quality of the action of the homœopathic remedy is determined by its quantity.*

22. Consequently, the *Law of the Least Quantity of Action* (MAXIMA MINIMIS) will have to be acknowledged to be the *posological principle of Homœopathy.*

CLINICAL CASES AND OBSERVATIONS.

THIRD SERIES.

Capable of being treated in the rigid manner of the positive sciences, and removed, by reason of the nature of the topics with which it is concerned, from the strifes of medical sectarianism, this noble subject can develope itself in silence, without disturbance and without restraint; and yet such an advance cannot take place without compelling a reflecting effect to ensue in statical physiology, and hastening the time, when, by the united consent of all physicians, it, too, will be cleared from every mystification, and brought within the pale of exact and positive science.

DRAPER.

Ὑγιανσις και νοσανσις ταυτον.

HERMIAS in Plat. Phaedr.

The following cases have been treated with High Dilution Potencies, prepared in the following manner: One or more globules of a given centigrade Potency were dissolved in a few drops of water, and about as much alcohol (94°) was poured upon this solution, as would give a volume of one hundred drops of alcohol for all together; from this Dilution globules were medicated in the ratio of one drop to ten grains. One or more globules of the so obtained Potency were then used for a second Dilution, and the same process was repeated a third time.

It will be seen, that this mode of Potentiation coincides with the one adopted by Jeanes, but it differs from that, by starting the first Dilution from a given centigrade Dilution Potency, and not from the mother tincture or saturated solution. According to my method, the refining process is considerably accelerated, and I understand, that Hahnemann pursued a similar plan in his later years.

The notation of these Potencies consists in fractional figures, the numerator indicating the number of globules given, the denominator the number of the Potency out of which the Globule Potency was prepared, and in the globule sign of Hahnemann $\circ$ with the Potency number above, *e. g.*, *Merc. v.* $\frac{2}{30}$ $\overset{3}{\circ}$, which means *Merc. v.* two globules of the third Globule Dilution Potency out of one or more globules of the thirtieth centigrade Dilution Potency.

CASES.

1. HÆMORRHOIDES ANI CŒCÆ.—Mrs. N., 30 years of age, of German descent, black hair and blue eyes, small stature.

December 12th, 1858. Complains since this morning of burning pains in the anus with protrusion of a varix as large as a pea, very painful on sitting upon. *Sep.* $\frac{4}{30}$ $\overset{2}{\circ}$.

This dose relieved the pain, as soon as it melted upon the tongue, "as if from an aura," (Hauch.) Patient also felt easy as if there was no protrusion whatever, which disappeared pretty soon altogether.

2. IRRITATIO SPINALIS.—Mrs. D., 30 years of age, American, black hair and blue eyes, of nervous temperament, middle size.

September 23d, 1856. Complains of pain in her left side as if she had lifted something heavy, and of weakness under her left shoulder-blade from fatigue. Her whole left side is weak habitually. The pain came on ten years ago, during pregnancy, and lasted till after confinement, when it went away for a short time. It then returned, and continued ever since. *Calc.* $\frac{6}{30}$ $\overset{3}{\circ}$.

October 11th. Patient felt much stronger, after that, and was decidedly improved. The pain was gone, and has not returned since.

3. RHEUMATISMUS ACUTUS.—Mr. N., a full-sized gentleman of German descent, 45 years of age, blond, subject to rheumatic attacks from time to time.

February, 1860. Was down very hard with inflammatory

rheumatism in his knees and feet, which were considerably swollen, red, and extremely sensitive to the least touch or motion. His susceptibility, by want of sleep and by pain, was increased to such a degree that when I had ordered *Bry.* $\frac{2}{30}$ $\frac{1}{c}$ to be given three times during the night, it was found that every dose severely aggravated his pains immediately after taking, and his wife remarked to me the next morning, "your medicine is too fine, it affects his nerves too much."

High inflammatory fever, continuing without intermission, caused me to order one drop of *Acon.* 1, to be given in one gill of water by the tea-spoonful. The first dose immediately brought on strong undulation of the heart and did not diminish the fever, on the contrary, the fever ran higher, and alarming delirium took place. Other low Potencies, *Nux v.* 12, *Bry.* 3 and 4, were of no better use. I then prepared and gave to the patient a dose of *Acon.* 2000 $\frac{1}{0}$ which cooled him off immediately, and then at short intervals of two or three hours, *Bry.* 10,000 $\frac{1}{0}$, $\frac{2}{0}$, $\frac{3}{0}$, which brought on, for the first time, rest and sleep. These Potencies were then administered in the further course of this case with marked beneficial effect, and patient got well.

OBSERVATIONS.

Ἡ 'ομοια ἡ ἀνομοια ἐξ ἀρχης.
HIPPOCRATES.

Nur das Gleich—Gegen heilt.
HERING.

Relating to these High Potencies, I beg to submit the following observations:

1. High Globule Dilution Potencies prove efficacious and curative in single doses.
2. They sometimes present the phenomenon of homœopathic aggravation, though, it would seem, in a lesser degree than the other High Potencies.
3. They, therefore, seem to be especially adapted to the higher grades of susceptibility of the organism, and also to those low states where aggravations are to be dreaded as lessening the chance of cure.
4. They, for this reason, are most valuable agents, to meet distinct

harassing symptoms in those cases, where the fund of life is oscillating towards sure dissolution.

5. These High Globule Dilution Potencies are very practicable in regard to their preparation, since a higher degree of fineness is obtained in a shorter time and with less labor and expense, than by Hahnemann's and Korsakoff's methods, especially if the proportions are enlarged in the inverse ratio, what Hering calls 'erweitern.'

6. The common mode of giving the pellets, by dissolving in gills of water, and by tea-spoonful, first introduced by Aegidi, is a preparation similar to these High Globule Dilution Potencies :—*Refracta dosis.*

7. The curative action of homœopathic remedies consists in the mutual action of remedy and organism, that is, of the drug in its proper selection and application and of the organism in its actual state and susceptibility: —*Mutuum.*

8. Mutual action consists of action and reaction, and they are always contrary and equal, under the third Newtonian Law :—*Contrariety and Equality of Mutual Action.*

9. *Mutuality of Action* is the *qualitative* character of all medical action.

10. For the purpose of effecting the cure, as the organism must be susceptible of the remedy, so the remedy must be susceptible by the organism and its concerning organs.

11. The susceptibility of the organism is varying and different in each individual case.

12. For this reason, it is necessary, to individualize the susceptibility as well as the dose and the remedy. (*Organon*, §§ 92, 95, 97.)

13. The susceptibility actually stands as the indication and measure for the form and quantity of remedial action required in the given case, *i. e.*, for Potency and Dose.

14. The correct judgment of the actual susceptibility in the given case implies not only the careful examination of the case, considering the morbid symptoms of the organism, in its present state as well as the ætiological symptoms of previous health and habit and disease, and including the physical method of inspection, palpation, pressure, succussion, percussion, auscultation, mensuration, chemical and microscopical investigation, and the like; but also the perfect knowledge of the mode of action and power of the medicine upon the healthy and sick organism, and its probable ratio to the organism in question, derived from the above elements, after having been eliminated.

15. The *Susceptibility*, therefore, serves as the *diagnostic* principle of Homœopathy.

16. Susceptibility depends upon Assimilability of matter in general. As the organism is assimilative to the remedy, so the remedy is assimilable by the organism, and *vice versa.*

17. *Pathologically*, as well as *physiologically*, life is conditionated by Assimilation, and it depends upon Assimilation in disease as well as in health, and as much was taught by Hippocrates.

18. Health and disease are not contradictory things, but, as has been observed by Hahnemann, Reil and Comte, contrasted forms and modes of existence, and contrary states of the same organism, and both are governed by the same laws.

19. Consequently, Pathology is the counterpart of Physiology, both being correlate to the given state of the organism and under the dominion of the same Laws of natural processes.

20. Therefore, in a physiological and pathological aspect, the healing process by High Potencies, in its modality, appears to be a *process of Assimilation*, the disease, as Hering expresses it, assuming the form of the remedy.

21. The *Law of Assimilation* serves as the *physiological* and *pathological* principle of Homœopathy.

22. Quantitatively, Assimilation is molecular, and depends upon the fineness and infinitesimality of matter and motion, both of the drugs and the concerning organs :—*Homœoleptomeria.*

23. Assimilation by the organism is quantitatively carried on, and mediated, by the elementary organs and imperceptibly fine and delicate conduits in the organism.

24. Accordingly, a corresponding fineness of the drug matter is required, proportionate to the assimilativity of the organs.

25. The crude and massive form of the drug is not such as to admit of the required assimilation.

26. The required fineness and assimilability of the drug-matter is obtained by Potentiation.

27. The quantity of remedy thus obtained is, necessarily, molecular and infinitesimal.

28. *Infinitesimality* is the quantity of remedy required for the action which is to be curative and to constitute the healing process, the remedy assuming the form of the disease.

29. Therefore, Infinitesimality stands as the indication and measure for the remedial quantity required for the curative process :—*Posological Endeixis.*

30. Infinitesimality is, in point of fact, the quantity of the homœopathic remedy :—*High Potency ; Minimum.*

31. Consequently, *Infinitesimality* is the *quantitative* principle of Homœopathy.

32. *Infinitesimalization*, or *High Potentiation*, and *Microdosia*, serve as the *pharmacological* principles of Homœopathy.

33. Qualitatively, Assimilation depends on the material nature and distinctive quality of matter and action, both of the concerning organs and the drug, and upon their specific relation to each other.

34. This quality and relation to each other, of drug and organism, in the healing process, must necessarily be the same with the nature of all matter and action in mutual action, that is, under the third Newtonian Law of Motion :—*Contrariety* (and Equality) *of Action and Reaction.*

35. Accordingly, the very nature and conception of a remedy or medicine consists in this, that it is opposed and contrary to the given state of the organism:—*Contrariety.*

36. Therefore, a drug, in order to be a remedy or curative medicine, is necessarily opposed and contrary to disease, when that is the given state of the organism, and equally opposed and contrary to health, when that is the given state of the organism:—*Contrarium.*

37. Consequently, every drug which is a remedy or curative medicine, is always a *medium*, *i. e.*, means of changing the given state of the organism into its contrast,—health into disease (*Nosansis*, *Pathopoesis*, *Pathogenesis*), and disease into health (*Hygiansis*, *Hygiopoesis*, *Pathoktony*).

38. This Contrariety is found, according to the above quoted maxim with which Hippocrates opens his book on the Physician's Office, by contrasting the similities and the dissimilities, that is, by contrasting the given states of the organism, as they are affected by the drug, which are contrary, and also the effects of the drug upon the organism in its contrasted states.

39. By so contrasting, the Contrariety is shown in the positive fact, that the effect of the drug administered upon the healthy is opposite and contrary to that of the same drug administered to the diseased, and, *vice versa*, that the effect of the drug administered to the diseased is opposite and contrary to that of the same drug administered to the healthy:—*Nosansis* ⇄ *Hygiansis.*

40. This Contrariety is the real character of the homœopathic remedies, and positively proved by experiment and experience, our Provings and Clinics, since Hahnemann invented and operated upon his ever admirable plan of pathogenetically testing drugs upon the organism in its healthy state.

41. This Contrariety stands as the indication and measure for the direction of the remedial action required for the Mutual Action of which the homœopathic healing process consists.

42. Therefore, *Contrariety* is the *pharmacodynamical* principle of Homœopathy.

43. In a *chemical* aspect this Contrariety, or opposition, is represented by the physical force, or property of matter, which is known to physical and chemical Science by the affirmative term of *Affinity*, which is the affinity of opposition between two different bodies and particles of different nature to one another, and depends, as Faraday states, upon the energy with which particles of different kinds attract each other:—*Molecular Attraction.*

44. The effects of *Affinity* are neutralization, as shown by Berthollet, and all cure, as observed by Hering, is conditionated by a kind of neutralization effected by Chemical Affinity between drug-matter and disease-matter.

45. Consequently, this Affinity and Contrariety represents, in fact, what Hahnemann called "*medicamentorum vires positivæ*", that is, the specific quality and relation to the organism of those substances which

are known as Homœopathic Potencies:—*Pharmacodynamical Specification; physiological, pathological and therapeutical.*

46. The proof for this fact is in the effects of these Potencies, which are contrary to the disease, the homœopathic Simile and Chemical Affinity being identical, as Hering states; and the evidence of it is in our *Materia Medica Pura*, confirmed by its counterpart, our *Clinical* experience.

47. It is a fact, that not every Contrarium is curative; because, as Hippocrates says, the most contraries are not the most contraries; and it is, therefore, for our therapeutical purpose, necessary, to find, which is the curative Contrarium in the given case.

48. This is to be done under the guidance of the LAW OF HOMŒOGENEITY, adverted to in the above maxim of Hippocrates, and which Hamilton affirms, but inaccurately names the Law of "Homogeneity," and which enunciates, that things the most dissimilar must in certain respects be similar:—*Principium Similitudinis.*

49. In order to find the curative Contrarium, we must follow out the Hippocratean rule, placed at the head of these observations, by comparing the similities, that is, by comparing the similar given states of the organism, as they are effected by the drug, and also the effects of the drug upon the organism in its similar states.

50. Hahnemann was the first who understood this, and acted upon the true understanding, when he compared the symptoms observed as the effects of disease upon the organism in its diseased state, with those which appear as the effect of medicine upon the organism when applied to its healthy state:—*Hygiansis* ∾ *Nosansis.*

51. By so comparing, it appears, positively, that the effects upon the organism of the medicine which is contrary to its given state, and the effects upon the organism of the cause of disease, are resembling or similar to one another according as applied to the one or to the other of the contrasted states of the organism, such effects being disease either way, and always correlative to the state of the organism:—*Simility; Parallelism of Symptoms; Semiological Resemblance of morbific and remedial action:—Hygiopoesis* ∾ *Pathopoesis.*

52. This Simility is the real and distinctive character of the effects of homœopathic remedies in relation to the effects of disease, and the same has been positively proved, over and over again, by experiment and experience, since Hahnemann first took up the true comparative thought of Hippocrates; and the evidence for it is in our Provings and Clinics:—*Ομοιον; Simile.*

53. *Simility* is the *qualitative principle* of Homœopathy.

54. Mutual Action is impossible between Contraries only, and also between Similars only, as Anaxagoras already observed; but it is possible, and really taking place, between Contraries and Similars, when acting together:—*Relatum.*

55. Consequently, Simility and Contrariety, together, form the fundamental relation between drug and organism, and govern the quality of

this mutual action in the healing process, and are, like health and disease, not contradictories, but correlates to and convertible into one another.

56. Both, Simility and Contrariety, are also, like health and disease, correlative to the state of the organism, and convertible into one another, and the effect of the remedy and the disease is always similar, and always contrary, to the given state of the organism, according as applied:—*Correlatum.*

57. Whilst a remedy, as such, must always, in *abstracto* or *a priori*, be *a* Contrarium, *in concreto* the Simile is always *the* Contrarium in the given case, because a Dissimile is not contrary to the disease *in concreto*:—*Simile Contrarium.*

58. The existence and reality of the correlation between Simility and Contrariety in remedy and disease, is proved by the fact, that symptoms appearing in the disease similar to those obtained by (medicine in) Provings in health, are unerringly, and with certainty, neutralized by the administration of that medicine which produces in the healthy the most similar symptoms (Org. § 50):—*Homœopathicity.*

59. This Homœopathicity, the immortal discovery of Hahnemann, is the medical property of every remedy, which is as contrastable, as comparable, in its effects to that *Pathema* or disease, which it is able to produce, and is the property by which it is capable of initiating the mutual action of the healing process, which it could not do, if it was not Simile and Contrarium and Correlatum at the same time:—*Homœopathology.*

60. From this results, as a logical deduction, the undeniable fact, that the same medicine or Potency makes and unmakes the disease, as the case may be:—*Similia Similibus Curantur.*

61. This is precisely the doctrine of Hippocrates, as he laid it down repeatedly, and with numerous illustrations, not to be misunderstood, if correctly and entirely read, and which is concentrated into these two sentences: *each* (disease) *has its own peculiar nature and process, and none is of an ambiguous nature or irremediable and the most of them are curable by the same means, as those by which they were produced*" (De morb. sacr.); and "*disease is produced by the similia, and by the administered similia, from being sick they get well.*" (De loc. in hom.)

62. Such is the true orthodoxy of Hippocrates, ignored by Galen and his followers, and which was touched upon by various philosophers, such as Anaxagoras, Arndt, St. Augustinus, Baco, de Verulam, Basilius Valentinus, St. Bernhardus, Boyle, Cardanus, Auguste Comte, Cartesius, Darwin, Democritus, Thomas Erastus, Benjamin Franklin, Fechner, Goethe, Haller, Lagrange, Leibnitz, Mill, Nikander, Ozanam, Pascal, Shakspeare, Tycho de Brahe, Zeising, Zimmerman, etc., and which, also, was, here and there, practically applied by professional physicians—*Homœopathia involuntaria,*—but scientifically and practically established and vindicated by none but our own Hahnemann.

63. The *Law* of *Homœopathicity* (SIMILIA SIMILIBUS) is the Law of Proving and Cure, or the *therapeutical* principle of Medicine.

64. *Logically* examined, this Homœopathicity is correct, and as far from being paradox, as the truth, that the same hammering makes and unmakes magnet, or that the same magnet attracts and repels.

65. The rationale of this Homœopathicity, as the combined result of the correlation of Simile and Contrarium, is found, not only in the very nature and conception of a medicine or remedy, which is, that it must be opposed and contrary to the given state of the organism, upon which it is to act, therefore must necessarily cause disease when applied to the healthy, and cure disease when applied to the diseased state of the organism (because only thus it can possibly be contrary to the given state in either case); but, also in the fact, that the pathematic effect of the remedy upon the healthy is similar to the pathematic effect of the disease upon the healthy in the given case:—Ὁμοιοπαθεια.

66. Since, as Hamilton expresses it, Relation and Correlation are mutually referred, and can always be reciprocated and converted, and since the healing process is a Mutual Action, neutralizing the disease; it is clear, that disease and cure, perturbation and restoration of health, ægrotation and probation, nosansis and hygiansis, pathopoesis and hygiopoesis, pathogeny and pathoktony, are relations which mutually imply each other:—*Metathesis, Conversion.*

67. Therefore, *Conversion* serves as the *logical* principle of Homœopathy:—*Contrariorum eadem est scientia.*

68. The Galenic school only contrasted the contrary states of the same organism, and only the effects of the drugs upon the diseased states of the organism. That method was necessarily incomplete, and gave incorrect results, being an imperfect comparison, and hence led to an erring diagnosis.

69. They failed entirely to realize, that, not only, one thing or action is similar to its parts or elements or to those of another, but that, also, two things or actions, which are similar to a third, are similar to themselves.

70. Hahnemann, however, was the first who comprehended this, and took the full bearings of the Hippocratean rule, and extended the comparison to different organisms, and to the similar states of them, as affected by the drug in proving and cure, and compared the symptoms obtained by provings with the symptoms caused by disease, and the symptoms removed by the remedy with those caused by health.

The comparison instituted in this manner, comprehends both Contraries and Similars, and this method is necessarily complete and correct, resulting in a true Diagnosis and Therapia.

71. The Hippocratean *Rule of Similities and Dissimilities*, or what Comte and Mill call the *Method of Comparison*, and which of old has been known as *Principium Similitudinis*, is the *philosophical* principle of Medicine.

72. By the Law of Homœopathicity, the given disease itself, in its symptoms, furnishes the endeixis of the remedy, and the remedy itself, in its symptoms, furnishes the diagnosis of the disease:—*Endeixis & Diagnosis.*

73. And *Simility* is practically the *endeictical*, theoretically the *inductive* principle of Medicine.

74. *Simility* is the generic term of comparation, comprising the different species of congruency, equality, equivalence, equipollency, and resemblance, under the general Laws of Resemblance which are scientifically appreciated by Mill, and which, from the beginning, have always been empirically used as the ever ready instrument for examining into the nature of all things and actions, and determining and arranging them for reference, or, in other words, defining their quality.

75. *Ratio* is the measure of the relation between two things or actions, considered as quantities with regard to their Simility.

76. Every two things and actions, as quantities, represent in their mutuality two equal ratios, the first one being to the second, as the second is to the first.

77. The equality of two ratios is a *Proportion*.

78. The property of all things, to be in proportion, in general, inasmuch as they are parts of the Universe, and in particular, inasmuch as they are opposed to each other by nature or experiment, according to a certain ratio, is *Proportionality*.

79. *Equality*, as the highest grade of *Simility*, stands as the indication and measure for the Proportionality of the Homœopathic Mutual Action, or for the qualitative selection of the remedy required for the assimilation which constitutes the healing process by Homœopathic High Potencies in a given case :—*Qualitative Homœopathic Endeixis.*

80. The Homœopathic Simility is *Proportionality*.

81. *Proportionality* is the *analytical* principle of Homœopathy.

82. On the strength of the actual correlation and logical conversion of disease and cure, pathogenesis and pathoktony, pathopoesis and hygiopoesis, nosansis and hygiansis, morbification and sanation, ægrotation and convalescence, are as little contradictories as the contrasted states of the organism of which they are predicated, but they are commutable and convertible terms, likewise and contrariwise applicable to the properties and forces of the organism and to the properties and forces of the medicine.

83. Consequently, a Potency properly applied to the organism must be, by its own nature, equally morbific and curative, pathopoetic and hygiopoetic, nosantic and hygiantic, pathogenetic and pathoktonic,—*medium* and *remedium*,—and it must exert its properties and powers as either, likewise and contrariwise, according as it acts upon and with the one or the other of the contrasted states of the organism in the given case.

84. Accordingly, the very nature and conception of a homœopathic remedy or Potency consists in that it is the "simile contrarium" related to and in mutual action with the diseased organism :—*Simile Contrarium Relatum and Correlatum.*

85. A High Potency is an infinitesimal quantity of such a remedy :—*Simile Contrarium Minimum.*

86. In the views here taken, it appears that the formula *Contraria Contrariis*, as applied to curative action, if any thing, is the converse of, and tantamount to, our formula *Similia Similibus*, and this is as much as was observed by Hering as early as 1826, and by Goeschel in 1832, and recently acknowledged by Grauvogl and Politini.

Either formula is much like a proverb which, somebody remarked, is a short sentence, grammatically saying one thing and essentially meaning another.

But both formulæ combined, avoid the ambiguity and make the formula more complete: *Contraria Similia Similibus Contrariis Curantur.*

87. This equipollency of both formulas of medical treatment, was indeed known to and appreciated by Hippocrates, in whose book *de locis in homine*, BOTH methods, that PER SIMILIA as well as that PER CONTRARIA, are laid down as being proper treatment, as both being "contrary" modes; and where it is stated by him, that "*the most contraries are not the most contraries*," and that "*as any body's nature is changed and perverted, complaints are produced and cured by contraries*," and it is emphatically added, that "*thus by* BOTH *contrary modes health is restored, and if it was the same in all cases, the matter would be understood, and thus these would be remedied by the contraries whatever they are, and by whatever they are produced, but these by the similars, whatever they are, and by whatever they are produced.*"

88. This doctrine of Hippocrates must be considered as an entirety, comprehending both the Contraria and Similia, alike, and together. This was disregarded by the one-sided expositor Galen, and his followers, who, by omitting the Similia altogether, as it were, left the part of Hamlet out of the play, and thus established a false orthodoxy in Medicine. The full extent of the Hippocratean idea was first correctly understood by Hahnemann. He, first of all, perceived and realized the truth, and the whole truth. Recovering the original ground of it, he founded the true doctrine, and, substantiating it practically and scientifically, he created Homœopathy.

89. From the preceding observations results our complete formula:

Maxima *Cantraria* *Similia*	*Curantur*	*Similibus* *Contrariis* *Minimis*

that is, SIMILIA MINIMIS CURANTUR.

90. And it results, that Homœopathy rests fundamentally on the general principles of *Simility*, *Contrariety*, *Proportionality*, *and Infinitesimality.*

CLINICAL CASES AND OBSERVATIONS.

FOURTH SERIES.

Major in exiguo regnabat corpore virtus.
STATIUS.

THE following presents a report of some cases treated with the High Globule Dilution Potencies, described in our Third Series, but where they were further refined by a refraction of the dose.

They were administered by globules in a powder of sugar of milk, and either taken dry at certain periods of time, or dissolved in one gill of water and taken by teaspoonful at stated hours. The solution made fresh every day, as a general rule.

CASES.

1. ENDOCARDITIS.—S. B., of New York, a girl five years old, of German descent, blonde hair and blue eyes, rather large for her age, was reported to labor under the following complaints:

November 19th, 1860. Three weeks ago patient had inflammatory rheumatism, which was treated allœopathically without success. About a fortnight ago, a hollow hard cough set in with pain in the pit of the stomach, weeping, turning red in the face, and scanty expectoration of thick white mucus, excited by crying and aggravated in the evening and night. Dread to cough. Difficult respiration. Short and loud expiration. Sleeplessness, jactitation, pains all over, heat in the nights, otherwise cool. Won't eat nor play. Urine red, turbid in passing. Large ring-worm at the right fore-arm and wrist, radial side. Bowels regular. Hooping cough prevailing in the neighborhood. *Verat.* $\frac{1}{2400}$ in each of two powders of sugar of milk, to be dissolved in one gill of water and one teaspoonful to be taken once in three hours.

21st, three, P. M. Patient was brought to the office. She was the two last nights extremely restless and delirious and complained much, especially of pains in the abdomen, chest and throat, when coughing. Cough less in frequency, of metallic sound, short loud expiration. Hands hot. Fever at nights with slight perspiration. Dropsical swelling of the face, abdomen and feet. Urine red, turbid and scanty. Cannot sleep in the recumbent position. Wants to be carried all the time, her body leaning forwards as much as possible. Peevishness. Pulse almost imperceptible. Distension of the chest over the region of the heart. Heart's action labored. The sounds of the heart are like the ticking of a distant watch; the first sound accompanied with a blowing noise at the apex which was found in its normal position. The ring-worm presents no unusual aspect. Patient received at once *Spig.* $\frac{2}{750}$ $\frac{3}{\circ}$, and was directed to take when at home *Spig.* $\frac{1}{750}$ in one powder, to be dissolved in one gill of water, one teaspoonful to be taken once every hour.

22d, ten, A. M. Patient got no sleep yet; had, however, more rest last night. She drank often water, but little at a time. Urine slightly increased in quantity, clear, brown like beer, and without albumen. Less dyspnœa. Legs very much swollen, especially one of them. Sometimes circumscribed red spots on the cheeks, sometimes a deadly pallor of the face; face last night cool. Same hard dry cough. Patient had a hard stool and passed about one pint of urine last night and this morning. Decided aversion against food. She wants to be carried on the arm, the body lying motionless against the shoulder of her mother, the head hanging down over it. Utter impossibility to lie down. The herpes itches intolerably and is very dry, the vesicles at the circumference being all dried up. Patient is so low that further examination must be dispensed with. *Lyc.* $\frac{2}{30}$ $\frac{3}{\circ}$ in each of seven powders, to be taken dry, one every night and morning

25th. Slept well last night. Fever gone. Stool normal. Urine copious and clear. Patient can now lie flat on her back. Got some appetite. Breathing natural. The chest presents no distension. The swelling of the legs increased November 23d, considerably, and then went down gradually to a slight swelling on the insteps. Very impatient. Coughing from passion. The herpes itches so much that she scratches it bloody. *Sep.* $\frac{1}{200}$ J. (Jenichen).

29th. Remarkably improved. The swelling is gone and she runs about.

December 9th. Patient called at the office. The heart presented nothing abnormal, except that the left side of the chest seemed a little fuller than the right one. The herpes heals up from the hand towards the arm; there are only a few scales left. Complains of sometimes pains under the navel in the abdomen, which is somewhat enlarged. *Merc. v.* $\frac{2}{30}$ $\frac{3}{\circ}$ in each of seven powders, to be taken dry, one every night.

After that the patient rapidly recovered and was healthier than ever before. It was reported lately, that she remained perfectly healthy ever since.

2. RHEUMATISMUS ACUTUS.—Mr. W., German, fifty years old, locksmith, robust, of dark complexion, and violent choleric temper, hard beer-drinker, sleeping regularly four to five hours; had many years ago a disease in his stomach which ever since had been weak. Dr. Epps of London, ten years ago, treated him successfully for rheumatism in the back. Patient suffered habitually from hæmorrhoids. It was about a month ago, at a fire, when he took cold from being drenched thoroughly with cold water after profuse perspiration. He used for it "all and every thing," also iodide of potassium which aggravated the case considerably, and applied mustard-plaster and plaster of turpentine and sulphur.

November 28th, 1860 ten, A. M. Patient is reported by his wife, to complain of the following symptoms: incessant lancinating pains in the right loin extending as far as the right knee and sometimes going to the back, worse on moving. If he tries to rise, he "cries aloud like a baby." After the exertion, profuse perspiration breaks out with the odor of iodide of potassium (taken in large quantities.) Tongue clean, but turning white during the most violent paroxysms of pain. Salty taste (cannot bear salt and farinaceous food generally). Thirst. Pale face. Urine clear and of strong odor. Emaciation. Want of appetite and sleep for the last eight days. Some pain in the chest. Cannot sit nor lie. Continual fever for the last two days. *Bry.* $\frac{3}{10000}$ $\frac{3}{\circ}$ in each of four powders, dry, night and morning.

29th. After taking the first dose in the forenoon, patient felt better in the afternoon, and, for the first time since over a week, slept for two hours soundly, when the pains woke him up again. At ten, P. M. (the second dose was taken at nine, P. M.), all of a sudden the pain became so violent as to make him faint; then followed some relief till morning. Right knee swollen. Tearing pains in the right thigh towards the knee, aggravated at the least motion. Had a stool yesterday morning. Flatus. Much thirst. Urine thick and red. Constant perspiration, but now without odor. *Bry.* $\frac{6}{10000}$ $\frac{3}{\circ}$ in each of two powders, to be dissolved in one gill of water, and one teaspoonful to be taken every third hour.

December 1st. Better. Fever gone. Slept well and got an appetite. Less perspiration. Bowels regular. Urine smelling strongly, thick and red like blood with red sediment. Moderate swelling from the right knee to the hip. When lying quiet on the affected limb he feels well, but on the least motion the pains return. *Bryonia* as above.

3d, nine, A.M. Can walk over the room now and can sit up for half an hour without pain. After the urine had a thick clayey sediment like rags, day before yesterday, it continued to be clear since. The pain is now stinging and jerking in the hip-joint as far as the knee. Much fœtid flatus. Patient used to smoke tobacco during the pains which started the flatus. Pain when lying on the painless side. *Rhus. tox.* $\frac{3}{10000}$ $\frac{3}{\circ}$ in each of six powders, to be taken dry night and morning.

7th. Took the first powder in the evening. The next morning he had violent pains in the head. It is reported now, that the taking of the powders in the evening always brought on severe pains in the affected parts for a while, but not so last night. Profuse sour perspiration last night. Feels much better this morning. The stinging is less, and only in the thigh; the hip-joint is entirely free. The thigh feels cold, like dead between the skin and bone with cold drizzling during the pains. Was up for half a day yesterday. Urine like beer. Much flatus. *Berb. v.* $\frac{2}{30}$ in each of six powders, to be dissolved in one gill of water, one teaspoonful to be taken once every third hour.

July 20th, 1860. From a gentleman who wanted my advice in a similar complaint, I learned that the patient was well ever since.

3. HOOPING COUGH.—P. H., of New York, a boy ten months old, of German descent. November 29, 1860. Had ever since he was born, a rough croupy cough, which was treated allœopathically, and since July, *a. c.*, assumed the form of true hooping cough, which was prevailing in the neighborhood. He has now coughing spells with rattling in the chest, hooping, vomiting of food and slime, want of breath, and turning bluish red in the face, worse before midnight. Constant restlessness. Sleeps very little. Very much gone. *Dros.* $\frac{2}{30}$ $\frac{1}{0}$ in each of fourteen powders, to be taken dry, one every night and morning.

December 9th. This helped him in a few days. The first day after taking the medicine, the stools were loose. The rattling in the chest and hooping cough disappeared. There is some dry cough yet on waking up from sleep which is disturbed. *Dros.* $\frac{2}{3000}$ $\frac{1}{0}$ in each of fourteen powders, to be taken dry, one every night.

August 17th, 1862. From a neighboring patient I learned that the cough shortly after the last prescription had all at once disappeared, and the child was well ever since.

4. RHEUMATISMUS ACUTUS.—Mr. G. B., of New York, of Irish descent, forty-six years old, laborer, middle stature,

dark blond, habitually suffering from irritation of the neck of the bladder, complained as follows:

May 29th, 1862. Drawing stiff pains in the left upper arm with inability to lift it, aggravation on moving, fever and uneasiness about the stomach. *Bry.* $\frac{2}{30}$ in each of four powders, to be dissolved in one gill of water, and one teaspoonful to be taken once every third hour.

June 2d. About the same. The pain is right in the bone at the head of the humerus, fixed and aching, running down along the bone of the upper arm, night and day. Both hands swelled considerably with thick veins. Pulse small and frequent, probably compressed by the swelling. Much fever. Urine dark colored. Applied a liniment which did him no good. Prostration. *Rhus. tox.* $\frac{6}{10000}$ $\frac{3}{\circ}$ in each of four powders, to be dissolved in one gill of water, and one teaspoonful to be taken once every hour.

9th. Patient began to feel easy as soon as he began to take that medicine, and wants more of it. Can lift the hand to the head now. Swelling gone. Appetite good. Arm worse on moving it. *Rhus tox.* $\frac{2}{10000}$ $\frac{3}{\circ}$ in each of four powders, to be dissolved in one gill of water, one teaspoonful to be taken every third hour.

September 19th. After that, patient reports, he got entirely rid of his rheumatism.

OBSERVATIONS.

> Now, since causes and things caused are similar to each other, although they differ in degree and dimension, it follows that nature is similar to herself, and cannot be different in the larger system or elementary kingdom from what she is in the lesser—in the macrocosm from what she is in the microcosm; in a volume, from what she is in a particle; hence in the elementary particle may be seen the quality of the volume, and in the volume the quality of the particle. SWEDENBORG, (*Principia*, Clissold's translation. London, 1845. Preface, p. xiv.)

In continuation of our observations on the process of healing by Homœopathic High Potencies, we beg to submit the following:

1. Homœopathic Globule Dilution Potencies are efficacious and curative, when administered in watery solution, or in refracted doses:—*Refracta dosis.*

2. By such prescription a further attenuation or refinement of the Potency is obtained, without reaching the terminus of efficacy.

3. In a *physical* aspect the mutual action which constitutes the process of healing by Homœopathic High Potencies, has been well noticed by Hering, to be illustrated by the process of *Interference* which is known and established, alike, in Optical, Acoustical, Thermological, and Hydrodynamical Science, (Clydonics).

4. The interferential process appears to rest upon the general principle for the mutual action of coinciding similar series or systems of motions, molecular, vibratory and oscillatory, by which, under certain conditions and at certain points they augment, at others diminish, and at others entirely destroy each other, producing darkness by adding light to light, silence by sound meeting sound, cold by heat overcoming heat, and rest by wave encountering wave.

5. Since the conditions for Interference are mutual action, molecular motion, simility and contrariety, and infinitesimal quantity, and since its effect is neutralization and conversion; it is clear, that the conditions and effects of Interference are the same as observable in the homœopathic healing process by High Potencies, and the analogy is obvious.

6. The *Law of Interference* serves as an illustration of the *physical* principle of Homœopathy.

7. Assimilation, physiological as well as pathological; and Affinity, chemical as well as medical; and Conversion, logical as well as remedial; and Interference, physical as well as therapeutical;—altogether, have in common the same elements and conditions, viz.: Mutuality of Action, Motion and change of motion, Simility and Contrariety, Molecularity, and Infinitesimality; and also the same effect, viz.: change of the given state, and neutralization, and mutual conversion.

8. The same common elements and conditions and effects, mentioned (*Obs.* 5), are observable to exist and take place in many other processes of nature, *e. g.*, in the *biological* (physiological and pathological) processes of absorption and resorption; ablation and apposition; alimentation and nutrition; digestion and congestion; arterialization and circulation; chylification and lactification; hæmatosis and cholepoesis; albumination and fibrination; excretion and secretion; exûdation and suppuration; irritation and counterirritation; contagion, infection and disinfection; thrombosis, coagulation and tuberculization; inflammation, ulceration and cicatrization; tumefaction and delitescence; induration and ossification; respiration, perspiration and transpiration; inhalation and exhalation; innervation and enervation; crescation and atrophy; eutrophy and hypertrophy; vaccination and syphilization; intoxication and paralysis; ovulation, fecundation and embryonization; incubation and gestation; generation and germination; domestication, breeding and crossing, etc. Also in the *botanical processes* of inoculation, gemmation, foliation, floration, fructification, vegetation, propagation, etc. Also in the *physical* (and *chemical*) processes of osmosis and capillarity; endosmosis,

exosmosis and diosmosis; absorption and resorption; allotropism, homomerism, isomerism, metamerism and polymerism; crystallization and granulation; aggregation, disintegration and catalysis;—vaporization, evaporation and condensation; solidification and liquefaction; congelation and colliquation; saturation and rarefaction; fermentation and putrefaction; carbonization and cineration; combustion and explosion; mixtion and distillation; solution, resolution and reduction; fusion and diffusion; undulation and vibration; flection, deflection and reflection; fraction, refraction and diffraction; radiation and irradiation; coloration and spectration; adhesion, cohesion and ruption; elasticity and expansion; deposition and incrustation; pulverization and precipitation; petrefaction and adipoceration; phosphorescence, fluorescence and calorescence; annealing and steeling; amalgamation and combination; oxydation and desoxydation; vulcanization and calcination; galvanization and magnetization; electrization and induction; telegraphy and photography; polarity and astasy. And also in the *general* phenomena of attraction, repulsion and gravitation; morphosis and amorphism; anamorphosis and metamorphosis; homoplasia and heteroplasia; accommodation and acclimatization; composition and decomposition; formation and function; determination and gradation; specification and variation; qualification and modification; production and reproduction; differentiation and development; and indeed, in all generation, degeneration, and regeneration, and in all organization, disorganization and reorganization.

9. In a general point of view, all such, and similar processes, appear to rest upon, and be governed by, one common principle which, if found, might scientifically be considered as a general principle, or Law of Nature.

10. Such principle seems to grow out of Grove's conception of the existing universal correlation of the physical forces of matter, supported by Berthelot and Faraday, and out of what might be called a *Polarity of Action*, as being discernible in all natural processes by the conditions and effects mentioned.

11. As such general principle, or Law of Nature, might be proposed *the Principle of the Mutual Conversion of Physical forces of Matter into one another*, *or the Equalization of Bodies according to the Ratio of their Assimilability*:—UNIVERSAL ASSIMILATION, OR HOMŒOSIS.

12. *Physically* considered, then, the homœopathic curative process of healing by High Potencies, appears to be such a homœotic process as described, being governed by the same conditions, and presenting the same effects, as all homœotic processes.

13. Equally, the homœopathic probative process, of producing by medicine disease in the healthy, appears to be a homœotic process, being governed by the same conditions, and presenting the same effects, as the cure, in the reverse.

14. Also, the homœopathic potential process, of preparing medicine by trituration, dilution, contact and otherwise, appears to be a homœotic process, being, again, governed by the same conditions and presenting the same effects, as all homœotic processes.

15. In fact, all processes of morbification and sanation, aegrotescence and convalescence, nosansis and hygiansis, pathopoeia and hygiopoeia, with or without medication, are homœotic processes and reducible to the same principle.

16. Accordingly the *Law of Homœosis*, (*Similia Minimis*) is *the biological* principle of Homœopathy.

17. In a *mathematical* conception, everything in nature has been always, since Heraclitus, Anaxagoras and Aristoteles, considered to be reducible to motion, and change of motion, and thus the system of man in its life must also be conceived to be constituted by certain motions and changes of motion, in certain forms, conditions, and relations.

18. For the same reason the different states and conditions, or forms of existence, of the organism; health, disease, and restoration of health, are reducible to certain motions, and changes of motion, in certain forms, conditions, and relations.

19. Consequently, every homœotic process, (and among them the process of healing by Homœopathic High Potencies,) necessarily, besides quality and relation, involves and implies quantity and form, modality and motion, and relation.

20. Therefore, Homœopathic, and indeed all Therapia, is really amenable to, and under the dominion of mathematical conditions and a proper subject for mathematical demonstration.

21. The *Laws of Motion* serve as the *mathematical* principle of Homœopathy,

22. Under these laws the homœopathic remedial process, probative and curative, is *geometrically* demonstrable, being, as Hering observes, comparable to the diagonal of two forces; and the *parallelogram of forces* is its geometrical illustration.

23. Since every organism is at the same time a mechanism, the homœopathic process in the organism is subject to the Laws of Mechanics, statical and dynamical,

24. In this aspect, since the sum of the physical forces of matter is always constant in the Universe (as was already remarked by Leibnitz, and latterly scientifically established by Helmholtz, and sustained by Faraday, and practically carried out by Mayer, Baumgartner, Tyndall, *a. o.*,) the physical forces of matter, in reality, are constantly exchanging and compensating each other :—*statical and dynamical Equivalence.*

25. Accordingly, that system of motions which constitutes the organism of man, presents in its actual state a natural oscillating equilibrium which is normal in health and perturbed in disease, and this is what was recently so well elaborated and applied to Medicine by Grauvogl :—*physiological and pathological Equivalence.*

26. Consequently, that process in the organism which constitutes the cure or restoration of health, as the converse of disease or perturbation of health, represents that compensation, *i, e.*, that equation, and converse of equation, of forces and motions of the organism, which is effected by

remedy, and is the restoration of the normal oscillating equilibrium of the organism by medical action:—*therapeutical, hygiantic, or hygiopœtic Equivalence.*

27. Likewise, that process in the organism, which constitutes the homœopathic probation, or perturbation of health, as the converse of cure or restoration of health, represents that compensation, *i. e.*, that equation and converse of equation of forces and motions of the organism, which is effected by remedy, and is the perturbation of the normal oscillating equilibrium of the organism by medical action:—*nosantic or pathopoetic Equivalence.*

28. Herewith the real character and criterion of a "*remedium*", which means, etymologically, the restitution of the *medium*, is shown to be in the similarly and contrarily pathopoetic and hygiopoetic quality, and quantity, and modality, of the drug, and in its equally similarly and contrarily morbific and curative relation to the organism, which is, in fact, our Homœopathicity.

29. In this regard *Equation* serves as the *analytical* formula for the homœopathic treatment and cure in its perfection:—*Homœopathic Equation;* HOMŒOMA.

30. The *Law of Compensation or Equivalence* serves as the *mechanical, statical* and *dynamical* principle of Homœopathy.

31. From this is deduced Grauvogl's *Law of the therapeutical Motion—Equivalence*, by him proposed as the *Law of Dose.*

32. Since there is in reality no sameness, (ὁμον) or absolute equality, of any two real things, and there can be no identity (ἴσον) in the aspect of any two existing forms, as Draper expresses it; real things, if compared with others, and if by such comparison appearing to be nearer to absolute equality than to absolute difference, can only be similar (ὁμοιον) to others, or to each other.

33. This fact furnishes the natural and correct answer to the vexed question, "what is the Simile?" by the etymology of Hahnemann's original "æhnlich" which is the German word for the Greek "ὁμοιον" and the Latin "simile." The word, according to Adelung's authority, recognized as such in Hahnemann's time, is as much as "angleich," Anglo-Saxon "anlic" or "onlic" (English "alike"), and in its signification opposed to "gleich," Anglo-Saxon "lik" (English "like"?), for which the Greek is "'ομον;" and it means, etymologically and literally, "onlike," *i. e.*, 'near on like,' somewhat "ὁμον," near to equal, and in a measure so, more or less equal.*

---

* The origin of the words "*similis*" and "*similar*" is by Bopp (Vergl. Gram., Berl. 1842, § 808) ingeniously derived from the Sanscrit root "*ma,*" referring to the Irish "*samhuil*" cf. Sanscrit *sama, similis,* English *similar, same.* Pott (Etym. Forsch. Vol. II. p. 395,) derives it from the Sanscrit root *mâ* (*metiri*) and brings it still nearer home to its real meaning when he says: "*simili* (cp. sam-mi-ta) is either verbal as *facili* (*what can be measured together*) or nominal as *humili,* from *sama, imâgon* (*simulacrum*)," so that it appears, that the very expression of our "*Simile*" originates in the ancient most perfect Sanscrit language, and relates to the notion of comparison from the beginning.

34. The great Wolff whose mathematical and philosophical works were used as text-books in Hahnemann's younger days, defines "*Æhnlichkeit*" (Simility) to be the accordance of that by which the things are discriminated by the understanding, and concludes, that similar things cannot be discriminated if they are not brought together either in reality or in the mind by means of a third thing as, *e. g.*, a measure.

35. In this sense, "*Æhnlichkeit*" or Simility, denoting Equality as the highest degree of Simility, admits a series of gradations, and this again is already in popular language indicated by the use of the comparative and superlative "æhnlicher, æhnlichste, *similius*, *simillimum*," *i. e.*, more similar, most similar.

36. Since there are many degrees and gradations conceivable between Inequality and Equality, as already pointed out by Mill and others, there are such degrees and gradations conceivable of Simility and Contrariety, which represent the gradations of Affinity, and indeed of all Homœosis, within the limits of Proportionality.

37. These gradations are determined by the quantity of action which applies, the least possible of it being sufficient to change the same into one another, and to increase or diminish each of them more or less.

38. This is again the principle, established by Maupertuis, to which we referred before, and which, in fact, seems to be the *Spiritus Rector*, or regulator, by which everything, and every motion in existence, is prevented from being and becoming identically the same or absolutely equal with any other, and by which everything, and every motion, when becoming comparable with others, is made or kept in this state of Simility and the given gradation of the same.

39. Consequently, all motions and changes of motion, here concerned, pathogenesis and cure, and all Homœosis, indeed, all motion and change of motion throughout the Universe, proceed by and are under the control of the Law of the Least Quantity of Action.

40. In this view the *Law of the Least Quantity of Action* (MAXIMA MINIMIS) serves as the *cosmological* and *metaphysical* principle of Homœopathy.

41. The degrees and gradations of Simility, and Homœosis, may be different in quantity, in modality, and in quality, and infinitely many of all such different degrees and gradations are conceivable.

42. Therefore infinitely many proportionate remedies, and as many proportionate forms and quantifications of remedies, are corresponding to the homœotic degrees and gradations which are represented by the varying Susceptibility of the organism.

43. For the same reason, in order to insure the curative effect of our remedies, we want to be prepared with infinitely many proportionate medical qualities and relations, known to be curative.

44. Only with such complete apparatus we would be fully able to meet all cases and to carry out the rule of individualizing Symptoms and

Remedy, Susceptibility and Assimilability :—*Medical Proportionality, pathopoetic and hygiopoetic.*

45. Such infinite variety of medical qualities and relations is furnished by the exact homœopathic provings, such as are already made and such as are continually being made, and may be made in all future time :—MATERIA MEDICA PURA ; PATHOPŒIA.

46. Equally so, for the purpose of insuring the curative effect of our remedies in all cases, we want to be prepared with infinitely many proportionate different remedial modalities, forms and quantities, and corresponding relations, that is *Potencies*, known to be curative in the given case.

47. Only with such complete ammunition we would be fully able to meet all cases, and to carry out the rule of individualizing the actual Susceptibility of the organism and the Potency and the Dose :—*Pharmacopoetic Proportionality.*

48. Such infinite variety of ammunition is to be acquired by preparing the homœopathic remedies in various modes and forms and quantities, and by infinitesimal or High Potentiation, so that they may be administered in various ways and different degrees of fineness, from the lowest to the highest, proportionable to the requirements of the given case :—PHARMACOPEIA PURA.

49. When being so prepared with such exact knowledge of the effects of the Potencies upon the organism in the healthy state, changing the same into disease ; and when being prepared with a full ammunition of Potencies for the application : then we are enabled to apply the Potencies to the organism in the diseased state ; and when that is done according to the principles of Homœopathy, proportionally to the requirements of the organism in the given case, then, and then only, we are certain of the effects of the Potencies upon the organism, changing disease into health, that is, of the cure :—THERAPIA PURA ; HYGIOPŒIA.

50. *Pharmacopœia* is the art and science of potentiating the drugs or preparing the medicines for application upon the organism so as to render them susceptible and assimilable by the same.

51. *Pathopœia* is the art and science of applying the Potencies upon the organism in the healthy state and thereby converting health into disease.

52. *Hygiopœia* is the art and science of applying the Potencies upon the organism in the diseased state and thereby converting disease into health.

53. Since all the motions, forms, quantities and relations, here concerned, are under the dominion of Mathematics, they must, and possibly can be submitted to calculation.

54. As they are altogether infinitesimal, the proper calculus for them required, seems to be the *Infinitesimal Calculus.*

55. As the invention of this calculus preceded, and, indeed, alone rendered possible, the high development of Physics and Chemistry as positive and exact sciences, so its proper application to Medicine would carry

medical science to a point of scientific exactness which it could not reach without Homœopathy and its High Potencies.

56. The *Infinitesimal Calculus* would serve as the *proper mathematical method of investigation and computation* for Homœopathy and for high-potential Therapeutics in particular.

57. Since all theory must rest on reliable facts, the medical quality and relation, as well as the remedial quantity and modality of the drug, is only to be found and secured by experiment, observation and experience, and for this reason, the Homœopathic *Provings* and their counterpart, our *Clinics*, are, and forever will be, the ground-work and only safe foundation of Therapeutics and Medical Science in general.

58. In conclusion, if it is moral, to do the most good and the least evil possible, to our fellow-men, then Homœopathy is the true *Ethics of Medicine.*

59. If it is the policy of Nature itself, to effect the greatest amount of good with the least expenditure of force, then Homœopathy is the natural and true *Medical Policy.*

60. If it is religious, to believe, and live conformably to the belief, in the harmonious and unique government of the Universe, whether personified, singly or plurally, or otherwise, then Homœopathy is the true and universal *Religion of Medicine.*

61. If it is the doctrine of christianity and the bible, to do unto others as we would be done by, then Homœopathy is the truly *Biblical and Christian Medicine.*

62. If the true regular practice is that which is supported by a correct theory, then Homœopathy is the true regular *Practice of Medicine.*

63. If the true theory is that which is resting on positive facts and exact observations, and borne out by practice, and in accordance with the laws of the Universe, then Homœopathy is the true *Theory of Medicine.*

64. If the true art of healing is that which is fully supported, and borne out by theory and practice, and in perfect harmony, accordance and conformity with the Laws of Nature and God, then *the only true, natural, rational and real System of Medicine is* HOMŒOPATHICS.

65. When this true system shall be appreciated by Physiology, Chemistry and Physic; when Du Bois-Reymonds' *beau ideal* of Analytical Mechanics of all biological processes, and Draper's high idea of Analytical Physiology, both of them subsumable under Newton's grand conception of applying the mechanical principles to all phenomena of nature,* shall be realized; and when the instruments of the higher Mathe-

---

* "Utinam cætera naturæ phenomena ex principiis mechanicis eodem argumentandi genere, derivare liceret! Nam multa me movent, ut nonnihil suspicere ea omnia ex viribus quibusdam pendere posse, quibus corporum particulæ, per causas nondum cognitas, vel in se mutuo impelluntur et secundum figuras regulares cohærent, vel ab invicem fugantur et recedunt; quibus viribus ignotis, Philosophi hactenus Naturam frustra tentarunt. Spero autem quod vel huic philosophandi modo, vel veriori alicui principia hic posita lucem aliquam præbebunt."—*Principia, Praefatio*, Op. om., Horsley, Vol. II. p. X.

matics shall be brought to bear upon the investigation and analysis of morbific and therapeutical processes; all of which may be done, the doubts of Comte and Mill to the contrary notwithstanding, according to and by the homœological principles and methods of Homœopathy and its High Potencies: then a true comprehensive and correct Biology, and the corresponding Therapia, will be accomplished, and Medicine, through the stadium of Homœopathic Comparative Medicine, will be elevated to the real dignity of a positive and exact Science, answering the highest conception of ANALYTICAL MEDICS.

CLINICAL CASES AND OBSERVATIONS.

FIFTH SERIES.

E pauxillis atque minutis.
LUCRETIUS.

THE cases here reported were treated with High Dilution Potencies of my own preparation, carried up by further dilution on a new plan. The notation is on the centesimal scale. Every thousand is denoted by the letter "*m*," e. g., *Apis mel.* $\frac{3}{42\text{m.}}$, means two pellets of the forty-two thousandth Potency of *Apis mel.*

The success obtained by these Potencies, not only confirms the observations made in the First Series, but also establishes the fact, that the action and efficaciousness of Homœopathic Potencies is not limited to 20000 or 40000—the highest made by Jenichen—but evident even in higher centigrade dilutions, as in the 42000 of *Apis mel.*, in the 50000 of *Nux vom.*, and in the 55000 of *Sepia.*

The question, then, where, by potentiation, the terminus of medical action for Homœopathic remedies is to be found, at all, is *still* an open question.

The experience in case number 8, settles the fact, that our High Potencies, and, more particularly, doses of a third Globule Dilution Potency of a 10000 centesimal Potency, preserve their medical properties, and exert their curative action, when prepared and prescribed in America, mailed in a letter to Europe, and taken at Dresden in Saxony.

In the observations subjoined we commence summing up. When the first series was published (March, 1860), Bœnninghausen did them the honor of noticing them, publishing a translation with glosses of his own, cordially approving and supporting the views advanced.* Now, before the last series reaches his eyes, they are closed forever. The great master of our art, the champion of true Homœopathy, the standard-bearer of High Potencies in Europe,—he is no more.

With feelings of gratitude I cherish, personally, the memory of him, who, by words of encouragement and assurance, strengthened my purpose, when I first professed Homœopathy. "Man kann Alles lernen," he said, with true Franklinian terseness.

But with deep sadness comes the thought, that his powerful aid should be withdrawn now, when we most need it, to put down the false prophets, criticasters, double-dealers, and disunionists, who by supercilious misrepresentation and disparagement of Hahnemann's labors, betray and endanger the good cause. Oh, that he were still with us in the coming battle, to be fought on the true ground of Infinitesimality, which is ultimately to decide, by the High Potencies of scientific truth, the final triumph of genuine Homœopathy! *Have pia anima!*

CASES

1. ANGINA, OPHTHALMIA.—Therese S., 7 years and 9 months old, of German descent, dark complexioned, at a time when diphtheria was prevalent in the neighborhood, presented the following symptoms:

December 28th, 1863, three P. M. High fever with dry, burning skin; aching in the forehead: maturating of the eyes, which stick together so that she can hardly open them; swelling of the throat on the left side, with pain in swallowing; nausea; pains in all her limbs; sent her one dose of *Apis mel.* $\frac{4}{42}$m.

December 29th. The fever had ceased very soon after taking the medicine. Otherwise she is about the same.

* "Allgem. Hom. Zeitung," Vol. 61, pp. 63, 134, 140, 159, 164.

December 30th. Much better. The swelling went from the left to the right side. Tonsils very red, swollen, looking as if scratched.

January 1st, 1864. Stench from the throat in speaking. *Lachesis* $\frac{6}{20\text{m}}$.

January 2d. The swelling goes down. Two days after she was well.

2. HERPES CIRCINATUS.—Same patient.

February 13th, 1863. Ring worm, red and burning, as large as a copper cent, under the lower lip, for a week. *Sepia* $\frac{6}{55\text{m}}$.

After that the eruption subsided within a fortnight.

3. INDIGESTIO.—Mary S., sister of the same, 10 years old, blond hair, blue eyes, short, fat.

December 7th, 1863. After eating potato-salad and pork, vomiting early in the morning in bed; diarrhœa with tearing pains in the bowels; sour taste; coated tongue. *Aluminium met.* $\frac{2}{24\text{m}}$. Soon relieved.

4. ANGINA, OPHTHALMIA.—Same patient.

December 30th, 1863. Headache, both eyes watering and latterly maturating. *Apis mel.* $\frac{6}{42\text{m}}$.

January 1st, 1864. Watering and maturating of the right eye; gum-boil. *Belladonna* $\frac{6}{40\text{m}}$.

January 3d, 1864. The right eye maturating yet; fever, red swollen cheeks; pain on swallowing in the throat on the left side, externally and internally; no appetite. *Apis mel.* $\frac{6}{42\text{m}}$.

January 4th. Slight fever in the night; slept but little; throat red, swollen; left tonsil swollen; pain on swallowing still; right eye maturating; no appetite; little thirst. After a day or two well.

5. HÆMORRHOIDES CŒCÆ. — Mrs. N., American, blond

hair and blue eyes, 30 years old; after the loss of a valued friend;

February 27th, 1864. Complains of aching in the lower part of the back, followed by blind piles with stinging pains; stool regular. Used to have piles when pregnant, which she is not now. Neck and shoulders rheumatic. She is unable to walk. Great depression of spirits. Took *Opium* 200 (Lehrman) herself without effect. After *Nux vom.* $\frac{2}{50}$m., in some sugar of milk, she got well and went the next afternoon some distance to church. She said, "it acted like a charm."

6. RHEUMATISMUS.—Ch. F., boy 10 years old, dark complexion.

February 4th, 1864. Rheumatic pain in the right knee on walking. *Bryonia 40 m.*, some pellets.

February 5th. The pain disappeared in the morning after taking the medicine, and returned in the afternoon. *Bryonia 24 m.*, some pellets.

February 6th. The pain was gone.

7. ABLACTATIO.—Mrs. B., of French descent, dark complexioned, well-formed, was, March 1st, 1864, delivered of a healthy child. She did not want to nurse the child, although she had nursed her previous children, and was in good condition to nurse again now.

March 4th. Breast very sore, swollen as far as the left arm; pressure and soreness in motion and on touch. The milk is running out. *Bryonia 40 m.*, some pellets, to be dissolved in about one gill of water, and one teaspoonful to be taken once in three hours.

March 5th. She is doing well. The swelling went down; but still the milk is being secreted and oozing out. *Pulsatilla 51 m.*, in solution as before.

March 9th. The milk is gone; the breast is quite natural. She has no more uneasiness about it.

March 14th. Patient called at the office, reporting herself perfectly well.

8. HERNIA INGUINALIS.—J. F. F., of Dresden, Saxony, 75 years old, fat, middle stature.

August 19th, 1861, during a walk, got stinging pains in the right inguinal region, shooting over into the right hip and the right thigh, with difficulty in walking. Coming home, he noticed a swelling just above the pelvis near the hip. After Aconite 30 it disappeared, but afterwards it returned. He then must pass water more frequently than usual. The spine is curved on the right side in such a way that, when sitting, the lowest ribs touch the right hip bone, the ribs having already assumed a corresponding curvature. Thereupon mailed him three doses. 1. *Nux vom.* $\frac{2}{5\text{m}}$. 2. *Nux vom.* $\frac{2}{9\text{m}}$. 3. *Rhus tox.* $\frac{2}{10\text{m}}$., to be taken dry, successively, one a week.

June 1st, 1862. Patient reports, that the remedies had acted successfully, when by a sudden and violent motion in bed he got a relapse. The next physician on hand was called in, and he declared, that it was an inguinal hernia, which, besides the bowels, contained also some omentum; he then reduced the hernia and put on a truss. Mailed a powder with a quantity of pellets of *Rhus tox. 10 m.* $\frac{3}{0}$* with the direction, to take three pellets once a week.

November 23d. Patient reports, that the hernia had no more protruded behind the truss as often as before, and that, whenever it occurred, it was hardly to be distinguished from a fold of loose skin.

April 3d, 1863. Mailed some more pellets of *Rhus tox. 10 m.* $\frac{3}{0}$, three once a week.

December 7th, 1863. Received the good news, that the hernia had come down no more, that there was no more any difficulty about it, and that patient had stopped taking medicine.

March 12th, 1864. Patient reports, that the hernia did no more protrude.

---

* High Globule Dilution Potency, see the Third Series, p. 28.

OBSERVATIONS.

> I approve much more your method of philosophising which proceeds upon actual observation, makes a collection of facts, and concludes no further than those facts will warrant.
>
> DR. FRANKLIN TO ABBE SOULIAVE.

It remains, to gather the consequences and proper deductions for General Science, to be drawn from the facts and observations collected in the preceding articles, and also to sketch the position which Homœopathy, especially as determined by High Potencies, deserves to occupy among the Sciences. But we must here limit ourselves to the following suggestions:

1. The High Potencies which form the basis of our observations, are fully known as to their preparation and elements, all having been carefully registered in our books, and the clinical effects of them having been taken from our journals. So, there is no mystery, nor uncertainty, about these High Potencies, and they, at least, claim immunity from the sweeping objections by which heretofore even Goullon, Meyer, and others, actually excused themselves from considering High Potencies at all.

2. The general principle of potentiating remedies appears to be a working out of the old theorema: *corpora non agunt nisi soluta;* and its practical idea is a rectification of the old-school *Acuition.*

3. From the views presented in the observations, it results, that homœopathic remedies are agents and reagents, and, more particularly, that they are as homœodynamic with the organism in its actual condition, as the organism is homœopathic with them in their proper application. Hence, when they are indiscriminately termed homœopathic, it is done tropically.

The organism, in its healthy condition, is by homœopathic remedies always similarly affected, as it is in its diseased condition affected by the disease, and it is always contrarily affected by them in either condition.

A further result is, that homœopathic drugs are, likewise and contrariwise, morbific and curative, pathopœtic and hygiopœtic, pathogenic and pathoktonic, pathic and antipathic, nosantic and hygiantic, according as they are applied to the given state of the organism.

Conformably to these views, the character of homœopathic remedies is always *pathematic*, and at the same time always *homœomatic*, and always *dynamic.* It might be aptly designated as equally *homœopathopoetic* and *homœohygiopoetic*, equally *homœopathogenic* and *homœopathoktonic.* Such, or a similar terminology would seem to be serviceable for a short-hand description of the peculiar and distinctive nature of medical *Homœodynamicity*, in which we recognize the basal principle of that Simility and Potentiation which were both discovered and established by Hahnemann, the true son of Hippocrates, the equal of Columbus upon the vast ocean of Medicine. These discoveries, being positive enrichments of Science, form his highest original merit, his *monumentum œre perennius!*

4. Inasmuch as the direction of the action of our remedies in relation to the organism, and its constituent or integrant parts, is in every case distinct and peculiar, and unerringly specific, as has been recently so well elaborated by Grauvogl; it is certain, that their effect is always specific in each individual case, where it is properly administered and proves curative; and in this sense a homœopathic remedy is a *specificum.*

But this would seem to be about all of what is tenable of the theory of the specificists and of the schools which enjoy the delusion of being orthodox. There is no such thing as a specificum for any generic class of diseases, unless it means only a generalization and abstraction of pathognomonic symptoms of single remedies.—*Organon*, 5th ed., § 147.

5. The specific direction of the several remedies or drug matters, compared with the equally specific direction of the several hypothetical nosopoeses, or disease matters, presents again a Simility, and, on account of it, another property of homœopathic remedies, which is recognizable in that they are *homœotropic.*

6. In relation to *Therapia*, the inferences from the views developed in the observations, do not here need any more explicit elaboration. Generally, these observations may contribute to a correct understanding of what Paracelsus described as the pith of our art, in these words: "Summum artis mysterium erit in *naturæ et remedii convenientis cognitione.*"

7. Inasmuch as each homœopathic remedy has, and, especially in its High Potencies, maintains its own and peculiar pathematic sphere, and its own pathognomonic character, reflected in the pathogenetic picture:—the old *Nosology* will not be sufficient for any thing else than a mere nominal index.

But a better system of Nosology, that is, a true and real Pathology or *Pathognosis*, might be built up on the basis of scientifically comparing, and contrasting, and carefully and cautiously grouping, the different symptoms of the different remedies according to the traits which they have similar and in common. This might be done by combining the true pathognomonic symptoms with cautious and correct generalization, in which already Hahnemann, Bœnninghausen, Hering, Lippe, Jahr, and others, have succeeded to a great extent. The nomenclature, then still desirable, would most naturally be taken from the names of the drugs which produce the same or similar symptoms; *e. g.*, Aconitism, Carbonism, Digitalism, Helleborism, Iodism, etc.

Such a Pathognosis would mainly depend upon the study of High-potencies, because they, as is confirmed by Jahr, "present the real, proper and peculiar characteristics of the remedy."

True, such Pathognosis would certainly presuppose considerable help from micrological, microscopical, anatomical, microchemical and other exact observations, finer than those hitherto made by physicists, chemists and physiologists. Yet, it may confidently be hoped, that, as Science and Art proceed in their onward march, they will, with a fuller appreciation of the throughout micrological character of *all* matter, and of *all* natural processes, find and acquire those finer methods and instruments which are required to elucidate, palpably, what Homœopathy has already commenced to secure by her experience and observations and by her operations with the finest substances upon the fine organization of the human body.

8. Inasmuch as the true *Remedium* is that drug which in quality, substance and effect, is *contrary* to the given state of the organism or its concerning organs, therefore capable of unmaking the disease in the sick, and making the disease in the healthy organism; and which, at the same time, in relation, quantity, form and modality is conform and equal, ergo *similar*, to the given pathopoesis or morbification, and most nearly so, and in the exactest possible proportion unto the quantity and form of the disease; and which is, therefore, *homœotic*, or capable of assimilating the disease; and inasmuch as the corresponding pathopœsis or morbific agent must be *equally homœotic* or capable of assimilating the drug or hygiopoesis: it is clear, that such a *remedium, necessarily*, is thorough, direct, positive, radical, and precise in its effect, and that any other drugs selected and administered after other theories, can only be more or less indirect, negative, palliative or alterative, and uncertain in their action:—*Positivity of Homœopathy.*

9. *The correlation of physiological and pathological Assimilation* in the view we have taken, will find its illustration in an examination into the effects of our best known remedies from which we select Arsenic as an example.

The pure metallic Arsenic undergoes no oxydation in the alimentary canal, is eliminated in its pure metallic state, and not poisonous. (See Schmidt and Bretschneider in *Moleschott Untersuchungen*, Vol. 6, p. 140.)

The arsenious acid, if taken in large and massive doses, terminates life more or less rapidly, and is one of the most formidable poisons.

The same arsenious acid is taken habitually and regularly, in small doses, by mountaineers, in some places, for the purpose of improving their "wind" and of preserving and bettering their general health. And there its effects are, that the people who make a regular practice of Arsenic eating, with certain precautions, grow upon it sleek and fat and red-cheeked, and their appearance improves generally. Likewise it is given to horses, cattle and hogs, for the purpose of fattening them up. And we are informed, that in the Styrian stud of the King of Prussia it is made a rule to give Arsenic to the horses. The Arsenic serves as a nutritious element.

The same arsenious acid is, at some places, taken regularly and in small doses, by persons who are connected with the manufacture of Arsenic, for the purpose of avoiding the deleterious effects of the fumes of the poison, and this is done not only with impunity, but with marked benefit, as it preserves their lives. Thus Arsenic serves as a prophylactic and at the same time as a remedy and a nutriment.

The same arsenious acid, if taken in infinitesimal quantities, cures such complaints as are similar to those produced by it in large doses. Thus Arsenic serves as a true *remedium*, and is one of the most efficacious remedies in our Materia Medica.

Arsenic, therefore, stands as full proof for the fact, that the same substance may be indifferent, poisonous, nutritious, morbific or curative, as the case may be; the effect depending upon the mutual action of the organism and the drug, according as it is assimilable in different degrees.

We are aware of the objection against considering arsenious acid as a nutriment, on the ground, that it diminishes the ordinary waste of the tissues and causes an amount of fat and albuminous substances, equivalent to the repressed carbonic acid and urea, to remain in the body and to increase its weight, when the animal receives at the same time a sufficient amount of food. (*Schmidt and Stuerzwage Jour., f. pr. Chem.*, 1859, Vol. 78, p. 373.)

But this objection rests on the narrow view which physiologists take of assimilation. The arsenious acid must be assimilated by the tissues in some way or other, if it is to diminish their waste. And, that it is so assimilated, is conclusively proved by the chemical test in post-mortem examinations.

10. Hippocrates already observed the *correlation of physiological and pathological assimilation*, and laid down illustrations, and rules drawn from it for practice, in various passages of the books which we have under his name. His views in this respect are concentrated in this sentence: "For any other thing is food to one and injurious to another." (*de morbo sacro. ed. Adams* 2, p. 843.)

But this, like many other good things, was mostly neglected by his epigones, and so it is, that the profession generally, even homœopathic physicians, still cling to the untenable definition of a "remedy" which assumes it to be unassimilable matter.

It must be acknowledged, however, that Falck, of the physiological school, refers to the difference in the effects of toxication as depending upon the dose and the state of the organism. But he, too, completely ignores what, before him and in the very same direction, was observed by Hahnemann, and others, and what might be well made available for *Toxicology*.

11. With that understanding of remedial action, which is adopted in our observations, Bœrhaave's, "*Idem remedium aliter afficit sanum hominem, quam aegrotantem*," and Hartman's, "*Corpus etiam aegrum longe alium ac sanum a medicamento effectum experiatur necesse est*," are easily reconciled and scientifically confirmed. Of course, the same drug operates differently upon different states of the organism. And by our Homœopathy it is proved, that it operates contrariwise as well as similarly.

Of the Holmesian witticism, "that, what is injurious to the healthy, must be injurious to the sick," it is hardly worth while to say more, than that it is, at best, an injury to Logic.

12. The famous sentence "τα 'εναντια των εναντιων 'εϛτιν ἰημαρα" or "*contrariorum contraria sunt remedia*," attributed to Hippocrates in the spurious book "De flatibus" (Kûhne's ed. Vol. I, p. 569), is after all conformable with the views here presented. It does not at all justify the inferences drawn from it by the school whose dogmas Hahnemann stigmatized as Allœopathy. On the contrary, the sentence corroborates the homœopathic doctrine of Hippocrates, inasmuch as it formulizes the one-half of that doctrine, viz.: the Contrariety, without denying the other half, viz.: the Simility, which is adverted to by him elsewhere. Only, we must properly understand the whole passage, to judge correctly the sentence concluding it. The author distinctly says: "that it is necessary to "know the beginning and the source of the evils in the body. For, as "soon as one knows the cause of the disease, he can *give* to the body "what is *agreeable*, because he knows the disease from the *opposite* causes, "and in this consists the healing art according to its nature. For instance, "hunger is a disease; the remedy against hunger is that what satiates it. "This is food, therefore, it is the remedy."

This explains the sense of the sentence. For, to reason with the author, and to analyze, hunger is the disease; hunger is known by the opposite cause of the disease, since "we know the disease from their opposite causes," and such is satiation. Satiation is the health. Satiation is known by the "opposite cause" of the health, and that is hunger. Now, food is known to produce satiation; food is known to allay hunger. Therefore, food is the opposite cause of hunger, *i. e.* satiation; and food is the opposite cause of satiation, *i. e.* hunger. This is the logic of the Galenic school.

If the author spoke sense at all, the solution is, that "food" is used in different meanings; first, in a positive sense, as something being added, and then in a negative sense, as something being subtracted. If food is the remedy of hunger, as the author says, it is entirely homœopathic, that is, it produces in the one case what it removes in the opposite case. It produces satiation in the hungry by being given or "added" to him, and hunger in the satiated, by being denied or "subtracted" from him.

What else, then, has the author done, than to prove food upon the healthy *negatively*, *i. e.*, what it would not do, and to prove food upon the diseased, here the hungry, *positively*, *i. e.*, what it would do? And what else is this, than homœopathic?

When the author found, that food would produce no hunger upon the healthy, that is, the satiated, he was naturally led to this doctrine of "opposite causes" and to its application for satiating the hungry, because, if food will not make the healthy sick, that is, hungry, it certainly makes the hungry healthy, that is, satiated. The "*opposite*" and the "*agreeable*" are clearly identified. The Allœopathic Contrarium is *a* Contrarium, but the Homœopathic Contrarium is *the* Contrarium.

Hahnemann proved *positively*, by giving or "adding" to the body various substances from the three kingdoms of nature (nutriments included), and it is from that positive experiment, that we have obtained the Materia Medica Pura.

Again: whosoever acknowledges as genuine the book on the Sacred Disease which contains the homœopathic idea, will have to rank the book "*De Flatibus*" equally high, when comparing the conclusion of the book on the sacred disease with the sentence above discussed.

In either sentence the same idea is expressed, the same spirit prevailing, and almost the same language used.

Galenus acknowledges both these books as genuine, and all his followers attached so high a value to the book "De Flatibus," that they took the above quotation as a shibboleth or dogma of a new orthodoxy, thereby ignoring or dissimulating the true doctrine. Now we see, how they have deceived themselves, and that their orthodoxy is an old error and a common logical blunder, and a false heterodoxy. They mistook particularly the true meaning of "*τα 'εναντια.*" They took *any* Contrarium to be *the* Contrarium, *i. e.*, the curative Contrarium. But, what is not positively certain cannot be entirely certain. Their Contrarium is not *the* Contrarium. Logic would have prevented their mistake.

And here we may say, that some competent Greek scholar, thoroughly acquainted with the scientific and philosophical progress of our age, should furnish us a new, true and faithful English translation of the works of the great Coan. Such would do more justice to him and to his homœopathic comprehension, than hitherto accorded by Galenic taskmasters.

13. In regard to *Biology*, our theory of Homœopathic High Potencies leads to the following views:

Nutrition is the result of *assimilation of nutritious matter*, contained in the particles of food, comminuted and refined by mastication and digestion, and combined with indigestible matter which serves as a vehicle to keep the nutritious matter in the required condition of fineness and comminution.

Nutrition is thus carried on by *potentiation* of nutritious matter in the organism, rendering it assimilable by the concerning parts or organs of the system.

Every part of the organism assimilates of the nutritious matter, presented to it in a variety of forms, whatever is affined to its own substance and nature, and required to meet its wants.

Consequently, any food which by such assimilation contributes to the self-preservation of the organism, is proper nutriment.

As there is an assimilation of nutritious matter, so there is an *assimilation of noxious matter*, and whatever does not tend or contribute, or agree to, or concur with, the self-preservation of the organism, is noxious to it.

The indigestible matter of the particles of food which, as a vehicle, keeps the nutritious matter suspended in a state of comminution or fineness, forms one source of assimilation of noxious matter, being itself comminuted and refined by the process of digestion, in such a manner, that its assimilation is facilitated, which again is *potentiation.*

The ingestion of poisons and drug-matter in a crude state, by their contact and chemical action upon the organism, forms another source of assimilation of noxious matter.

The ingestion of nutritious matter, when nutrition is deranged, forms a third source of assimilation of noxious matter, the nutriment, thus ingested, itself becoming noxious to the organism, by virtue of its chemical and physical properties.

The perversion of nutrition, taking place where the self-preservation of the organism does not require nutrition, and being contrary to self-preservation, forms a fourth source of assimilation of noxious matter.

The ingestion into the healthy organism of drug-matter in a condition of comminution or refinedness, obtained by High Potentiation, forms a fifth source of assimilation of noxious matter.

All this taken together, it will be perceived, that *all* matter assimilated by the organism, through its various parts and organs, stands in the signification of nutriment or noxious matter, conversely, as the case may be. And, whether it act as the one or the other, depends upon the place, and upon the part in the organism, where the assimilation is going on, and upon the velocity of the assimilating process, as well as upon the (infinitesimal) comminution, or fineness of the matter, and, of course, upon the affinity of the assimilating particles to those assimilated, and *vice versa.*

Noxious matter may be assimilated, and by nature prevented from exerting its specific action, by being enveloped with indifferent tissues so as to remain indifferent or innocuous to the self-preservation of the organism for a longer or shorter time:—*Innoxious assimilation of noxious matter.*

Assimilation, everywhere, is accomplished by *Potentiation*, that is by rendering the infinitesimal particles of matter susceptible and active according to their inherent affinities.

Disease originates in the specific action of noxious matter which is either produced within the organism or brought in from without, and it is always carried on by a process of assimilation.

As homœopathic remedies are obtained by potentiation, that is by comminuting and refining drug-matter, by means of a *vehicle* easily assimilable; so nutritious matter appears to stand as the vehicle in the natural potentiation of those noxious materials which the organism itself prepares as remedies for its own self-preservation.

As the whole organism draws upon digestion, as the source of its nutrition, so every part and particle of the organism draws upon the various materials successively worked out by the different processes of animal chemistry for its own proper nutriment, and assimilates them for its own particular use and subsistence. Thus, the lacteals draw upon the chyle prepared by digestion; the lymphatics upon the transudation of the capillaries; the blood upon the fluids of either of these; and the nerves upon the blood.

Those parts of the organism which do not satisfy their wants and requirements by this intra-organic nutrition alone, assimilate from the outer world, whatever is necessary, not only for their own existence, but also for their co-operation with others and for the self-preservation of the organism. Thus, the blood assimilates oxygen from the air; the eye light; the ear sound; the nose olfactory matter; the tongue gustatory matter; the skin surfaces; the brain and nerves phosphorus; the mind operations of other minds by means of the senses, and so on; the organism, in fact, continually assimilating from the planet and the Universe as long as it lasts. Consequently, the whole organism is the product of Assimilation of matter, and its action is the result of Potentiation of matter. And so is disease. And so is health. And so is all life.

The hypothetical ether is, possibly, infinitesimally comminuted matter in space, forming, as it were, the reservoir of the High Potencies required for the *Universal Assimilation or Homœosis*, which is continually going on and mediating all life in the world.

The means by which this universal process of Homœosis is carried on, individually and collectively, are the Imponderables, as well as the Ponderables, and Gravitation, and indeed all natural agencies in turn.

14. The inferences for *Aetiology*, to be drawn from the above advanced biological views, are easily understood.

Inasmuch as the properties and effects of homœopathic remedies are similar to the properties and effects of what we must conceive to be the causes of the diseases which they cure, it would not seem unlikely, that the material substance or nature of both, the drug-matter and the disease-matter, should be also similar.

And, if so, it would give an important addition, if not a new basis, to Aetiology, which, therefore, will have to direct its attention to the Homœópathic Materia Medica, and complete its investigations by the results of the homœopathic provings which are, in fact, as many ætiological studies.

The probative process is the reverse of the curative process, and there is no reasonable doubt, but that by proving the disease is produced under the same Laws of Nature under which the disease is produced otherwise.

15. The *homœotic hypothesis* proposed in the course of our observations and deductions, is an unpretending effort of harmonizing, and subsuming under one common head, many important physiological and physical phenomena, which appear to bear near relation and resemblance to the healing process by Homœópathic High Potencies.

It can hardly be denied, that the homœotic nature of our healing process shows itself in the fact, that the remedies, in different degrees of Potentiation, exert their natural selection and affinity for certain parts and conditions of the organism in different degrees of intensity and Susceptibility.

Considering, that the conception of Mutuality of Action is, indeed, as Herbart observes, transferable and applicable to Chemical Affinity; believing, that the character of our Homœosis corresponds to Heraclitus' *Enantiotropia* and to Anaxagoras' *Diacosmesis*, and to Kepler's *Harmonia Mundi* and to Newton's *Delight of Nature in transmuting everything into its opposite*, and to Leibnitz' *Harmonie Préetablie;* and remembering Kant's conception of *Chemical Interpenetration*, which Herbart once thought, deserved to be made the foundation of all Natural Philosophy: we may feel assured, that further examination will be accorded to this subject for the purpose of more fully elucidating its comprehensive relations to Science, and that it will ultimately lead to good practical results.

As it is, our Homœosis presents a generalization and combination of Newton's *Attraction*, of Grove's and Faraday's *Universal Correlation and Mutual Conversion of the Physical Forces of Matter*, and of Herbart's *Concursus Incompletus*, applied to Physiology, Pathology and Therapia.

The homœomatic idea in general is proverbially expressed in Pope's sentence:

"All nature's difference makes all nature's peace;"

and poetically rendered in the lines of Tennyson:

"Nothing in this world is single;
All things, by a law divine,
In one another's being mingle."

It is classically depicted by Gœthe's master hand in the words:

"Und es ist das ewig Eine,
Das sich vielfach offenbart,
Klein das Grosse, gross das Kleine,
Alles nach der eignen Art,
Immer wechselnd, fest sich haltend,
Nah und fern, und fern und nah,
So gestaltend, umgestaltend,
Zum Erstaunen bin ich da!"

And it is, with characteristic emphasis and precision, embodied in Faust's exclamation:

"Wie Alles sich zum Ganzen webt,
Eins in dem Andern wirkt und lebt!"

But the practical realization of this homœomatic idea, and its application to Medicine, is properly due to Homœopathy.

CLINICAL CASES AND OBSERVATIONS.

SIXTH SERIES.

'Αι μικραι δυναμεισ μεγαλασ τασ ροπασ 'εποιησαν.

ISOCRATES.

The following report presents a further collection of cases cured by High Dilution Potencies of the description given in the First Series.

In the observations we continue the corollaries, commenced in the Fifth Series.

CASES.

1. B., a boy of German descent, six weeks old. October, 16th, 1861. Oval, elastic, bladder-like tumor in the right part of the scrotum, and moveable under it, as large as a pigeon's egg, sometimes larger, more like a small hen's egg. When the tumor is as large as that, patient spreads his legs apart. No testicle can be found at the right side. The veins injected at the surface of the scrotum at the right side. The tumor was never found to go away or to decrease, on the contrary it lately has increased so as to draw the mother's attention to it. The tumor offers an elastic resistance to the touch, without pain, and cannot be reduced. There is some eruption of small red pimples about the body and the mother is covered with larger red pimples all over. *Silicea 14 m.* one pellet.

October 25th. After that the tumor gradually decreased. The testicle became distinct and the tumor receded, above along the course of the spermatic cord, presenting a soft and roundish appearance.

November 5th. The tumor is entirely gone. Only now

and then there is a slight appearance as if the right spermatic cord was a trifle larger than the left one.

Also this symptom disappeared.

2. K., a boy of American descent, six months old.

June 1st, 1863. Hydrocele as large as a pigeon's egg. *Silicea 14 m.*, six pellets.

The tumor disappeared in two or three days.

3. DYSENTERIA CRUENTA. ALEX. R., five years, American, of German descent, very lively.

October 5th, 1864. Had yesterday ten, to-day fifteen bloody mucous discharges. Thinks he must sit all the time on the vessel. Tenesmus. Abdomen bloated, hot; griping pain about the navel; awful pain when bending over, and when passing stool. All over the body spots with thick reddish brown scabs with a small red base. He passed pure blood yesterday and two days before.. No passage without blood since the third of this month. Two, P.M., *Merc. v.*, $\frac{2}{10}$m., and *Merc. v.* $\frac{2}{6}$m., one powder to be given after midnight.

October 6th. Four, P.M., had a natural stool at one, A.M., at eight, A.M., but less, and ten discharges since; passes now more slime, when to stool, but don't like to get up again; less pain. *Merc. v.* $\frac{6}{6}$m., in one gill of water, one teaspoonful once in two hours, four powders.

October 20th. After three, P.M., he was all right; then he got a "tremendous appetite."

4. ASTHMA. Mrs. S., twenty-four years, of German birth, brunette, good natured.

July 12th, 1862. Tickling cough and asthmatic difficulty; want of breath, possibly from sympathy with her husband who is troubled much with Asthma in clear weather. *Puls. 7 m.*, in watery solution, every two hours, one teaspoonful. The second day she got a thick red eruption, very much like measles, all over the back and chest and the upper half of the upper arms. After a few days, whole pieces of skin peeled off. When I saw her a day or two afterwards, there were whitish brown scabs of pea size, and smaller, to be seen, which easily scaled off. The people thought it so strange, that they expressly came to the office, to show it to me.

Cough and asthma were gone.

5. DÉPILATIO. B., seven years, a girl, American, blonde, and brown eyes.

October 1st, 1863. A bald spot, as large as a dime, on the left side of the fore part of the head, and another one like it, as large as a pea, on the middle part of the head. Pains in the forehead, over the root of the nose. Had sore ears when a babe, and was treated homœopathically. Last January hives all over like erysipelas, and also treated homœopathically. *Thuj. occ.*, $\frac{5}{5m}$.

June 25th, 1864. "After five or six weeks the hair came in beautifully." Verbal report.

6. BLENNORRHŒA OCULI. A hen.

December 12th, 1863. Blenorrhœa of the right eye, with swelling of the right ear. *Euphras. off.*, $\frac{6}{2100}$.

December 13th. Better; in a few days well.

7. SCARLATINA MILIARIS. St., boy, eight years, American, of German descent, small and stout.

October 18th, 1863. Since the 16th he complained, first of his head, then of his belly, then he went to bed. Worse since yesterday afternoon. His mother gave him yesterday morning infusion of Senna, which produced a slimy diarrhœa. Then an eruption broke out, which, with the exception of the face, covered his whole body with red granules, very red and dense, especially at the trunk. Strawberry-tongue, violent fever, anxiety, with hot red face; inclination to delirium, worse in the warm room; a small place in the pit of the stomach extremely tender to the touch. Had three months ago hooping-cough, for which *Moschus* had been given to him; since then he "has it" in his head, he cries, and runs away, complaining of pain in his head. *Apis m.*, $\frac{2}{1}$m., in one gill of water, one teaspoonful every two hours.

January 27th, 1864. The fever did not last even a week; he complained no more; ran about in a few days, and the skin scaled off after a fortnight.

8. SCARLATINA LAEVIS. A girl, two years, child of the patient with Scirrhus mammæ, in the case First Series, No. 29, page 14, *ante;* of good appearance.

January 21st, 1864. Since a few days, some cough; yesterday high fever; red cheeks, red spots on the left cheek; teething; smooth, scarlet eruptions on the whole body, except in the face; tongue thickly coated, with the papillæ shining through; perspiration; sub-maxillary and parotid glands swelled. *Apis mel.* $\frac{2}{1}$m., in water every three hours. The child got well, without further development of the disease, in a few days, and the people said, it had not been scarlet-fever, though they had no doubt about it before.

9. VARIOLOIDES. P. G., eight years, poor constitution, American, of German descent.

October 31st, 1861. Came home yesterday from school with vomiting; delirium. Three, P. M., *Bell.* $\frac{3}{30}$, in water, every two hours.

November 1st. This morning vomiting of much slime; some cough; talking in sleep is usual with him; stands all the time crooked. *Ipec.* $\frac{2}{30}$, in water, once in two hours.

November 2nd. Since yesterday, an eruption breaks out, mostly in the face, on the arms and legs, less on the trunk, like small-pox, without pit in the centres. Pat. was vaccinated in the dispensary as a child, and had one good vaccine-pustule. Slept all night; less fever; urine brown; until yesterday afternoon all the excretions went from him involuntarily. *Thuj. occ. 5 m.*, in water, once in two hours, in one powder.

November 3rd. Talking much in the night. The whole

body is now covered with pustules; otherwise lively. Continued *Thuj. occ. 5 m.*, as above, one powder.

November 6. The pustules are quite full, and partly confluent; great photophobia; urine clear; violent itching of the skin.

November 7th. The pustules open.

In a few days everything healed up without further trouble.

OBSERVATIONS.

> It is the destiny of Homœopathy, not only to effect a glorious revolution in the art of healing, but to lead to new views of the constitution of matter.
>
> JOSLIN. (*Principles of Homœopathy*, 1850.)

The general observations commenced in the Fifth Series, are continued as follows:

1. It may occur to look for an explanation of the Homœotic Process by some higher law.

Some of our homœopathic systematists have introduced *Magnetism* (Altschul) and *Electricity* (Goullon), as a cosmological basis for the homœopathic quality of our remedies.

The high character of Science which we all claim for Homœopathy, warns us to be very cautious, and never too willing in adopting a bold, however ingenious speculation, when there are not yet facts enough to justify it.

The true nature and relation of Electricity and Magnetism will be better understood, when the idea of Potentiation shall thoroughly take hold of the scientific mind. This idea is like a powerful telescope, apt to dissolve the nebulæ of the so-called Imponderabilia, which even Liebig now styles "Potencies."

The facts and observations at our disposal as yet, are hardly decisive enough, to warrant us in assuming, that the quality of homœpathic substances, individually, is *proprie* magnetic or electric, or that our healing process is a magnetic or electric process, properly speaking.*

---

* By means of a most delicate Galvanometer I find that the human body conducts Galvanism as readily as a copper wire, though with more or less velocity and intensity, according to the state of the organism at the time being.

By means of a most delicate astatic needle, I find that the human body deflects the needle as an ordinary magnet does, differing or varying according to the sex, and part and condition of the organism, at the time being.

This would seem to indicate, that the chemical action in the organism produces galvanic

But whether or not the substances themselves, certainly their action, in relation to substances of the organism, may exhibit something like polarity and *Polarity of Action* might, indeed, be taken for a property common and essential to all Mutual Action and to all homœotic manifestations.

There is a general signification of the term *Polarity*, here applicable, by which it is used, to designate opposite or *dissimilar* properties or powers, simultaneously developed by a *common* cause in opposite or *contrasted* parts. And in this sense Polarity is a phenomenon observed, not only in magnet, light and electricity, but also in Homœosis which embraces them all. Not, that the matter concerned in the mutual action is itself polar, but that the Polarity appears to be in the motion and action of the matter concerned in the mutual action.

With such a conception of *Polarity of Action*, as being the property of *all* Mutual Action, it would seem, that in the homœopathic healing process the action of the remedy is polar to the action of the disease and *vice versa*, and that the convertibility of pathopœsis and hygiopœsis has its analogy in the *Exchange of the Poles.*

2. Referring to Obs. 13 in the Second Series; it must be remembered that every medication, as well as nutrition, and motion in general, follows the *Law of Contact*, which is in close relation to the nature of the bodies. What, of old, is called "*Impenetrability of the Bodies*," depends actually upon the reactive property common to *all* matter and force, that is, it depends upon Mutual Action. And this is effected always by Contact, the subtleties of the Leibnitzians to the contrary notwithstanding. For, as Newton says: "to suppose, that one body may act upon another at a "distance through a vacuum, without the mediation of anything else, by "and through which their action and force may be conveyed to one "another, is to me so great an absurdity, that I believe, no man who has "in philosophical matters a competent faculty of thinking, can ever fall "into it."

Now, in the said observation only dry contact is mentioned. But the Law of Contact is exactly the same with fluid substances. In fluids the infinitesimal particles, constituting them, are so arranged, that they among each other preserve their contact in such a manner, as to easily displace each other in all conceivable directions, without undergoing disintegration. A solid may be conceived to become a fluid by being potentiated, and equally so, by the same process a fluid may become a gaseous body being possessed of another kind of fluidity. (p. 26, *ante.*)

---

processes which, in their turn, again cause the magnetism observed through the astatic needle.

Persons possessed of much Animal Magnetism or Mesmerism, (Hahnemann Organon, 5 ed., § 293, 294,) deflect the needle more than those having less of it.

This shows, that Mesmerism and Animal Magnetism are identical with mineral and common terrestrial Magnetism.

These facts are directly practicable for application in probative and curative treatment.—(See Scientif. Amer., Vol. VI., p. 342, new series.)

If fluids act at all, they must act by Contact, just the same as gaseous or solid bodies. This is, what in Mechanics is expressed by the term "*Solicitation.*"

These views are in accordance with the *Theory of Contact or Continua*, adopted and cultivated by the best Mathematicians, especially by Lagrange, Poisson and Cauchy, and which has furnished fine results, but which was abandoned by its adherents, because they could not make out the phenomena of the so-called Imponderabilia. (Redtenbacher, Dynamiden, p. IV.)

Now, here, with our High Potencies, are positive facts, making out how Imponderables are produced by a known process of Potentiation, from measurable, ponderable and palpable substances. Was, then, the Continua-Theory so very wrong?

Homœopathics furnishes facts and proofs for it; the ignorance of them led to its being discarded.

Resuming this theory now, we find that, since the most simple relation of bodies to one another is that of Impact, the most simple *Law of Impact* would exactly tally and correspond with the *Law of Contact*, Impact being only another and a more definite term for the same thing on the one side, which is Contact on the other side.

The almighty shock which Newton postulates for the movement of the heavenly bodies, may well be supposed to consist of infinitely many little shocks, through an infinity of time and space, in all possible directions and with infinitely varying intensities. A hypothesis of this kind would, perhaps, enable us, reasonably to account for the great original shock, and its effect, by the conception, that the Infinite Impact is continuing all the time, bearing along everything and ourselves, too, with all our Philosophy and Mathematics, infinitesimally and infinitely.

3. The term "*infinitesimal,*" *i. e.* infinitely little, having been applied to Homœopathic High Potencies, it is to be distinctly understood, that infinitesimals are not infinites, and that Homœopathic High Potencies, too, are by no means infinites, but that they are finite quantities, real infinitesimals and infinitesimal realities. They are proved to be something, by facts of experience, and by logical induction. Hitherto their quantity has not been "assigned," that is, specified or designated with precision, and thus it is correct enough to call them infinitesimal, that is, of less than "assignable" quantity, which means less than hitherto has been or could be assigned *i. e.* precisely specified.

But it cannot be said, that they are less than "assignable," because it is impossible to assign their quantity. Only, we have to learn and find, that, and how, they are assignable.

In the mean while, and until the High Potential Calculus shall be established, all we physicians have to do, is, to show by facts and experience in our Healing Art, that the High Potencies *do* act, and do act with forces analogous to other forces of Nature. The results thus obtained will, after us, be taken up by the other proper departments of Science, and the Infinitesimals will be all the same, whilst the assignability of quantities will be realized and increased.

4. As applied to High Potencies, the Homœopathic Infinitesimal Dose is the medicinal quantity which, by virtue of its mutual action with the organism, is sufficient, to cause that specific hygiopœtic or pathopœtic motion, which, again, is sufficient to its purpose as a *Minimum* in the given case.

When the High Potency (always provided that it be homœopathically correct) is actually applied, the path which it has to pass through in the organism, and the time in which it does so, and the expenditure of force on the part of the organism at the time, will be the least possible, whilst at the same time the velocity of its action will be the greatest possible; and hence, the *Quantity of Action* necessary to effect either change, (Hygiopœsis or Pathopœsis) will, necessarily, be *the least possible.*

Whoever considers the size of the quantity of the homœopathic remedy employed in a High Potency, in comparison with the size of the quantities which the organism and its various organs oppose to it; and who ever will measure, weigh and number, estimate or calculate, as quantities, the symptoms of disease cured or produced by the least dose; will satisfy himself that the practical rule of *Maxima Minimis* is perfectly reliable for hygiopœtic and pathopœtic motions, as well as for all other kinds of motion.

5. The calculations periodically ruminated by enemies of Homœopathy, about Homœopathic High Potencies, for the purpose of ridiculing them as absurdities, are simply ridiculous. But, as they treat them seriously and gravely, we have to repay the compliment.

The argument made by them fails in the premises. These allœopathic philosophers fancifully create their own premises, and then take the figment of their own brain as a basis for their *deductio ad absurdum*, instead of taking, as a starting point, the plain true facts in the Process of Potentiation and using them as the basis of the calculation or as premises for the ratiocination.

It is natural, that such as are habitually looking at things superficially, are easily misled and deceived by the plausibility of a "proposition," and by the seeming exactness of a "calculation." Equally natural it is, that such as are constitutionally afraid of ridicule, should allow their sensibilities to interfere with their better judgment. But all this cannot alter facts, nor justify logical blunders.

Honest men of true scientific attainments are not so easily led off, by fibs, from the point in question, and they do not fail to see, in this matter, that the ridiculing calculators bravely fight a Quixotic battle.

The famous reasoning of these calculators starts from a self-made figure, and is based upon an arbitrary assumtion, which is this, that a little substance is, by potentiation, gradually magnified, according to its rarefaction or attenuation, to such dimensions, as the size of Saturnus, of the Sun, nay, so terribly large, that the whole planetary system would not sufficiently convey the idea of its magnitude.

The absurdity of the syllogism is evident. But the assumtion itself is totally wrong in fact, and a misrepresentation of Hahnemann's Potentiation-Theory.

Such magnifying is impossible by their own showing: how can Hahnemann be made responsible for doing it? It appears strange, that such an imaginary thing as this *magnifying* process would be, should be used as an argument against the *infinitesimal lessening* which is the gist of our Potentiation, as if infinitesimalizing were impossible, because its very contradiction, the magnifying, is impossible!

It might be fairly expected, that the very possibility of such lessening of a substance to such a remarkable degree, (as their own calculation would show in the converse), and which is already established as a fact by our Potentiation, would excite admiration of the greatness of Nature, and of man's mental power, to perform such a prodigious task by the simple means of a few vials, a small quantity of inert powder, an indifferent fluid, and comparatively little labor.

But, oh! that would be too plain and sensible a thing. They rather admire a thing for its impossible magnitude; they rather believe a thing, because it is absurd; and they rather disbelieve a thing, because it is beyond their comprehension.

That they should do so, is physiologically, and psychologically, explainable by muddle of brain and consequential confusion. But, it is, nevertheless, a shame and a pity. A little bit of logic, just a homœpathical dose of it, or even as much as those gentlemen themselves understand to be a homœopathic dose, would have prevented them from perpetrating such nonsense, as that is, to assume to prove, that, what Hahnemann did, is absurd, because it is beyond their comprehension, and that what he did is impossible, because it would have been impossible if he had done it otherwise, or done something else.

Only think of mere "Nothings," (of their own showing), so large that the world could not hold them!!! And, yet, that is their great gun.

Another circumstance here to be noticed is, that these task-masters arrive at their stupendous result by way of a calculation, limited to simple Arithmetics. They are in blissful ignorance of the fact, that simple Arithmetics alone are insufficient for Progressions, Proportions, Variations, and Potencies, which call for Higher Mathematics.

Thus, it is, that their appeal to common sense utterly fails, and their *argumentum ab impossibili*, turns on a humbug. *Job* XIII., 4, 5.

Dalembert once took a flask of water from the table, shook it up violently, until innumerable bubbles formed, and then said: "*calculez moi cela!*"

Well, why do not these aristarchs of Medicine calculate their own doses and their effects upon the same principle imputed to us? They take any quantity of drugs, and mix, and shake, and bottle, and shake again, forming innumerable bubbles,—why do they not calculate that? Every one of the substances taken for their drugging, is, itself, the result and product of innumerable previous attenuations and solidifications and substances and processes,—why do they not calculate that? The very effects of their drugs are innumerable indiscriminate bubbles in the organism, innumerable motions, and changes of motion, of innumerable infinitely little parts of the system,—why do they not calculate that?

"*Calculez moi cela!*" Can it not be done? Is it impossible, absurd, then, by your Logic, to prepare and use such drugs?

When our censors of the Galenic persuasion shall have done their calculations by the method on which they rely against us, they will be welcome to their criticism, including witticisms and all. It will thus be seen, what their *deductio ad absurdum* amounts to. In the meanwhile their sneer comes with bad grace from them, and we can afford to wait.

Our High Potencies are something more than that water and those bubbles in Dalembert's flask, and their preparation is something more exact than that chaotic shaking of Dalembert's; and hence the calculation of our High Potencies is something more practicable, than that of allœopathic medicine and Dalembert's "*cela.*"

The true method for such calculation may not be known yet, but does that prove, that it never will be? The ridiculers had better employ their acumen to Biological Mathematics, in order to assist in discovering the true MEDICAL CALCULUS.

6. Since the Fourth Series was written (1860), Kirchhoff and Bunsen published their paper on "Chemical Analysis by observations of the spectrum." (*Pogg. Ann.* Vol. CX., p. 161.)

This Spectral Analysis is actually a process of Interference. The waves of the solar light, coinciding with the waves of unequal length of the light of incandescent particles of metallic vapors, which are supposed to come from the solar atmosphere, interfere and produce the dark lines of Fraunhofer. A similar process of Interference is experimentally effected, when a solar beam is thrown upon the spectrum of a less luminous flame containing similar incandescent substances as are supposed to exist in the solar atmosphere. Here the less luminous flame with the incandescent substances represents the solar atmosphere. The substances artificially introduced are indicated by bright lines of different color in certain localities of the flame-spectrum, and correspond to those substances contained in the solar atmosphere, indicated by Fraunhofer's lines. Now, by Interference with the sunlight, the bright lines of the less luminous flame-spectrum are converted into dark ones, owing to inequality of wave length. Their precise coincidence with the original dark line of Fraunhofer, proves, almost beyond doubt, that the sun contains, in an incandescent state, similar substances as our planet.

The analogy of this Analysis to Homœopathy is obvious. It appears in the Infinitesimality of Action, as well as in the Convertibility of the contrasted states of the spectrum into one another. The fact, that the lines representing the contrasted states of the spectrum, are by the same agencies converted from darkness into brightness and from brightness into darkness, corresponds exactly to the fact, that the symptoms representing the contrasted states of the organism, are by the same remedies converted from health into disease, and from disease into health.

The light, as reflected in the spectrum, would represent the organism, and the bright and dark lines in the spectrum would represent the symptoms produced in the organism, by certain substances in infinitesimal quantity, in virtue of their specific relation to the organism. The Fraunhofer lines, being the normal state of the *solar* spectrum and restored by the solar light, would mean, that one given substance producing symptoms of disease in the healthy organism is neutralized by another similar one coinciding, which produces symptoms of health in the diseased organism, where the susceptive power is strong enough to admit of it at all. If the power of the organism is lowered, as represented by the less luminous flame, the substances burning in it with bright lines, produce symptoms of disease according to their specific relation to the organism; and, especially, if those substances burn on their own account, being present in the telluric atmosphere (Sodium, etc.), they stand for natural disease, and if they are artificially introduced into the flame (Lithium, etc.,) they stand for artificial disease—our Proving. By the experiment of Hahnemann, as well as by that of Kirchhoff and Bunsen, the qualities of the substances experimented on, are elicited, with the only difference, that what in Spectral Analysis are lines, in Homœopathy are symptoms; in other words, we find by Kirchhoff and Bunsen's experiment the physical, by Hahnemann's the medical properties of the substances.

These very substances which produce bright and dark lines in the same locality of the spectra of sun and flame light, convertibly, and as the case may be, are applied by us in proper Potentiation to the organism as remedies, when we direct the sunbeam of health upon the less luminous spectrum of disease. The substances producing disease in the healthy, are neutralized by Interference, as it were, of the similar substances producing the lines in the (solar) spectrum of health—here Potencies, as well as there, though differing in degrees—and thus by the same remedy the morbid symptoms, like the bright lines, disappear together with what is abstractly called disease, and the normal symptoms, like the Fraunhofer lines, are restored together with what is abstractly called health.

Quantitatively considered, this new Analysis furnishes new evidence for the efficaciousness, directness and specificness of infinitesimal action of attenuated substances, and already have Ozanam and others, taken its bearings upon the Homœopathic Potencies. In fact, this Analysis proves again the correctness and general applicability of the Maupertuisian Law of the Least Quantity of Action, and that Infinitesimality, which we claim as the quantitative principle of Homœopathy.

Qualitatively considered, it is another evidence for the correctness and general applicability of the Newtonian Law of Contrariety (and Equality) of Action and Reaction, and of that Mutuality, which we claim as the qualitative principle of Homœopathy.

But, it is not less striking as an illustration of the Correlation and Conversion in which we recognize the rational character of all homœomatic processes, including Interference, and which we claim as the logical principle of Homœopathy.

And, inasmuch as this Conversion is here demonstrated *ad oculos*, and verified, to take place really, and physically, and unerringly so, under certain conditions; and inasmuch as in this new Analysis again the same elements and conditions (Motion and Change of Motion; Simility and Contrariety; Molecularity and Infinitesimality), and the same effects (change of the given state, Neutralization and Conversion) are observable, which we find to be common to all homœomatic processes: this important and beautiful discovery elucidates and confirms the correctness and general applicability of the principle of the Mutual Conversion of Physical Forces of Matter into one another, and that HOMŒOSIS which we claim as the physical principle of Homœopathy.

7. Inasmuch as by the preparation and effects of Homœopathic High Potencies, it is proved beyond controversy, that by variously comminuting, attenuating, rarefying, fining and refining, crude drug-matter, growing

"Fine by degrees and beautifully less,"

certain properties of matter are not only kept and preserved, but also propagated, reproduced and improved, which are not perceived in the state of crudity; and that by the administration of so subtiliated substances certain matter of the organism is unerringly affected: we may safely concede, that by Potentiation the remedies are rendered molecular, and represent *molecular forces*, setting free, as Grauvogl has it, molecular motion, and molecular life, which were latent and unperceived in the crude state of the drug-substances. *Anamorphosis, Metagenesis.*

And we may also infer, that, as Assimilation is a molecular process, so the proper condition of a homœopathic remedy for being curative, is *Molecularity*, and that Potentiation is a process of *Molecularization.*

If we herein do not adopt Goullon's phraseology of *atoms* and *atomization*, we only give up his nomenclature, because that would imply absolute simplicity and indivisibility of the constituents and thus exclude the very idea of motion, and composition, which is belonging to molecules and indispensable for any theory of Potentiation and for Goullon's own.

8. Inasmuch as our own experience, conformably with that of Hahnemann, Aegidi, Burkhardt, and others, places it beyond doubt, that Homœopathic High Potencies exert their action unmarred and undisturbed for a long time, as well as immediately after their preparation, and as soon as they are brought into proper contiguity with the organism: we have again evidence of the identity of the curative action of these Potencies with the action of Chemical Affinity, because a very peculiarity of the latter is known to be, that it is capable of either waiting or acting at once (Faraday).

9. Lehmann says: "from the anorganic chemistry it is known, that the ablation or apposition of a single atom may conditionate such entire difference of properties in a single composed body; why, then, shall it still seem to us so very strange, when in the organic composition, where, on the whole, atoms use to group variously with such facility (isomeric), such changes are produced by a plus or minus of one atom?

This relates to Isomerism; Chemical Science knows also Homomerism, Metamerism and Polymerism.

But homœopathic experience would lead directly to an investigation of *homœomeric* bodies and *Homœomerism*, and it might, for such purpose, prove of interest, to refer to the Anaxagorean Homœomeria.

And, in so far as Allotropism is acknowledged to be another similar property of matter, also pointing to the facility of acquiring new properties by a mere infinitesimal change, the greater strictness of homœopathic observation would induce us to judge, that in the action of homœopathic drug-matter, as well as in that of disease-matter, a certain *Homœotropism* is perceptible, and that such, in fact, constitutes one of their properties.

10. Inasmuch as self-preservation, propagation, reproduction and improvement of its kind, are an undoubted criterion of organic life; it may be inferred, that Homœopathic High Potencies, like the constituent and integrant parts of the organism, are organic and organized matter, living micro-organisms, each with an individual existence, which, comparable to Milton's spirits,

> "that live throughout,
> Vital in every part, not as frail man,
> Cannot but by annihilating die."

11. And, inasmuch as no terminus of annihilation of homœopathic remedies by potentiating has been reached as yet, our High Potencies are new testimony for the *Imperishability of Matter*, always maintained by Hahnemann,* which, since his time, was successfully sustained by Moleschott, and has now become the very basis of research in Natural Science. "Matter, however, subtiliated, is matter still," (Boyle). And "material substances can neither be created nor destroyed, and the distinctive qualities which appertain to them remain forever unchanged," (Draper).

This is the great truth, so beautifully illustrated by Du Bois Reymond in his celebrated Preface, that it bears repeating: "A particle of iron is and remains assuredly one and the same thing, no matter whether it is

---

* "A substance distributed in ever so many parts, must still ever contain in its least conceivable parts something of that substance yet, and the least conceivable part does not cease to be something of that substance, and, therefore, it cannot possibly become nothing." (Organon, 5th ed. p. 288, Note.) Logically speaking, this amounts to the *Principium Identatis*. If a = a, it can never be = b, or = c, or =ↄ, everything being equal to itself, and to the whole of itself and of its parts.

propelled into space in a meteoric stone, whether it thunders along upon the railway in the wheel of a locomotive, or whether it pulsates through the temples of a poet in a bloodcell; as in the mechanism by the human hand, so in the latter case, not anything has acceded to the properties of that particle, not anything has been removed therefrom; those properties are from eternity, they are inalienable, intransferable."

Truly, a Homœopathic High Potency, in the language of Pope:

> "Lives through all life, extends through all extent,
> Spreads undivided, operates unspent."

12. It is an object of further investigation, how much of this preservative and reproductive organization of the drug, and of the medical properties, in the potentiating process, is to be attributed to the mode of *Preparation* (trituration, dilution, contact, succussion, etc.) and how much of it to the *Vehicle* (sugar of milk, alcohol, water, etc.)

Probably, the vehicle serves as the medium, menstruum or means, for keeping the remedial matter in the state of fineness required, and thus for facilitating its assimilation when required. At all events, here again is Homœosis observable, this time as mutual action between drug and vehicle.

13. It is, likewise, a matter of further inquiry, how much of the effects of Homœopathic High Potencies is to be attributed to the *Velocity* of the assimilating process in space and time. For the purpose of an instantaneous and perfect cure, *ceteris paribus*, the *momentum* of the remedial force must be similar to that of the pathopœsis or morbific force, that is *homœorrhopic*, the facility of assimilation standing as the measure of the susceptibility of the organism, which is found and elicited by individual examination in each given case.

The velocity and intensity of the hygiopœsis or curative force are mutually governed by the action of the organism, as well as by that of the drug, and the curative action must therefore be *homœotachic* and *homœorhythmic*.

And, by comparing this action with the known velocities of circulation, light and electricity, in nerves and in other bodies, we might, possibly, get at an approximative estimate, and infer, whether the effect of the remedy is in the given case conducted through the circulation, or the nerves, or how?

In any case, however, the LEAST *momentum* possible, because sufficient to cause a change, is certain to be all that is necessary to overcome the opposed force of the pathopœsis and to neutralize the same, as is always done by the mutual action of a cure or hygiopœsis.

14. Inasmuch as by the established effects of Homœopathic High Potencies it is certain, that the substance of the drug, after its refining or potentiating, is more pointed and more specific in its medical action, than the crude substance, or in Jahr's words, that "High Potencies present

the peculiar characteristics of the remedy," it may be assumed, that they exist and act under the dominion of the great *Law of Development*, first pointed out by Goethe, and, as Draper remarks, somewhat obscurely enunciated by Bähr in the following words: "the heterogeneous arises from the homogeneous by a gradual process of change," by which is meant, that in the process of development the stages are not from forms degraded from a higher type.

This gradual change is clearly homœotic and depending upon Leibnitz' *Law of Continuity*.

And, inasmuch as Development, to continue with Draper, is a Differentiation of a higher order, or a Compound Differentiation, and by Differentiation is meant an increase involving modification of fabric and the assumtion of new properties (symptoms): there seems to be no objection to the idea, that the process of Potentiation, and also that of healing through High Potencies, are processes of *Differentiation* and *Development.*

15. And if, agreeably to Draper's further observation, the great result of every Development is Heterogenesis and Homogenesis, only apparent as the conditions bringing on Differentiation approach Simility; we may adopt and apply this here, with the modification, however, that, in strictness and reality, it is not exactly Homogenesis, but *Homœogenesis*, which becomes apparent. Nothing can express this better, than the spiral whose curves are true asymptotes, ever tending to approach each other, but never meeting. (Rentsch, Homœogenesis.)

And here, and in this sense of Differentiation, and Development, with assumtion of new properties, we understand, corroborate, and justify, Hahnemann's often misrepresented theory, that the medical and scientific characteristic of Potentiation consists in the "*Kraftentwickelung*" or *Dynamization, i. e.*, development of force.

16. Besides quantity, quality, and relation, there is also the modality, and form, or the *morphological condition* of the drugmatter, as well as of the constituent and integrant parts of the organism, concerned in the mutual action of the curative process, and also, perhaps, the morphological condition of the hypothetical disease-matter, or pathopoësis. They present further important elements for analyzing the nature of the matter which is mutually active in the healing process.

Microscopical observation, in this regard, has not yet given us sufficiently many of certain and positive facts, because the fineness of the object is so extreme, that it still escapes perception by the instruments now in use; and hence the effects of our Potencies, as perceived in the organism, are still the only means of observing them. This morphological condition, therefore, deserves further attention. Stereoscopic observations would help much.

Thus much, however, upon comparing the said effects in the given case, might be safely assumed, that the motions and functions, proper to the remedial matter, are in form similar to those of the pathopoëtic matter, and that the constituent and integrant organs or elements, and their motions and functions, as concerned in the mutual action of healing or diseasing, respectively, are in form similar to the substance, motions and functions of the remedial and morbific matter, respectively, that is, that they all are *homœomorphic.*

Equally plausible it is, that all these matters are in a similar condition of fineness in particles, and proportionate in form to each other, so as to admit of susception and assimilation, that is, that they are *homœoleptomeric.*

17. Inasmuch as *Homœomorphism* presents a legitimate scientific point of view of our subject, legitimate inferences may be drawn from it. Among such might be one in regard to those strange and interesting indications for discovering peculiar remedial properties, in organic and inorganic substances, by their certain peculiar form and appearance, which from old are known as *Signatura Rerum.*

Superstition is connected with this subject, as it used to be with Astrology and Alchemy before the scientific development of Astronomy and Chemistry. But the subject never fairly died, and Helig, and recently Granvogl, bestowed their attention to it.

Now, it would not be unnatural, nor supernatural, to think, that,—because every thing, and every organ, consists of a certain system of motions and functions, peculiar to it, and unique of its own, and adapted to the intent for which it is existing and formed,—the regularity and object of such functions and motions, causates and conditionates, by the plasticity of nature, a certain configuration and form in the thing, or organ, which appears to the eye and acts visibly. The organic form is always a result of the operation of the substance. And if it could be made out, as may be done by a conception of the *Homœoplasticity of Nature*, that such functions and motions, and the inferred configuration of the parts constituting the thing or organ, are homœomorphic: then simility of configuration, *Homœoplasia* and *Homœoschematism*, would be an expression and conception of what is commonly called *Signatura Rerum*, and it would explain, how, really, such *Signatura*, as the effect of the homœoplastic forces of Nature, might serve as indication of certain medical properties, and that they, if correct, can only be homœopathical, and that they can only be correct as such, if homœopathical.

18. Since there are in reality no two things identical (ἴσον) and no two diseases identical; there can be in strictness no isopathic remedy, and *Isopathy* is impossible by nature and by logic.

The substances which are improperly called isopathic, are products of the organism in certain diseased conditions; and whilst there is no question as to their efficiency *in praxi*, there is no doubt, that, *when* curative, they are *homœopathic* remedies. Such substances represent, incorporate, and typify, in their formation, the whole complex of the disease from which they result and which is their pathogenesis. Upon this positive ground they may be properly applied against similar diseases and formations; but it will always have to be done with certain precautions, as for instance, that the isopathic substance to be used, be taken from individuals presenting the disease, or pathema, in a most simple and uncomplicated form, and that it be subjected to the process of Potentiation.

When regular homœopathic provings of those so-called isopathic substances shall have been consummated, *lege artis*, as has been done already with Hydrophobine, Psorine, etc., by Hering, Stapf, Gross, Redm. Coxe jr., and others; then we shall have most valuable additions to the Materia Medica Pura, and probably arrive at a fuller scientific explanation of their medical action.

19. Whether the remedial and the pathopoëtic matter in mutual action, might be also similar in respect to the parts constituting either, is another question offering itself for speculation. Generally speaking, the observed simility of both, the drug and the disease matter, in form, quantity, quality, properties, and effect, seem to allow an inference, that both might also be composed and constituted of similar parts, that is *homœomeric*.

And, even the Anaxagorean conception of Homœomeria would confirm this in a measure, because, if everything consists of similar parts compared with itself, those things which are similar to each other, must also have a simility of their constituent parts as compared with each other.

But this question pertains to the department of chemical science which will decide it, when it shall at length avail itself of the homœopathic facts, and when, taking a homœomatic view of the matter and giving to Potentiation its due credit, it shall be able to develope its higher branches into *Metachemics*.

20. From the preceding spicilegia it would seem, that the substances which we know to be homœopathic remedies or Potencies, as conceived in their mutual action with the organism, are homœodynamic and homœpathic, homœopathogenetic and homœopathoktonic, homœtropic, homœomeric, homœorrhopic, homœotachic and homœorhytmic, homœomorphic, and homœoleptomeric, homœoplastic and homœoschematic, and consequently *homœomatic* withal.

21. All these several properties and effects taken together, seem to warrant the further conclusion, that they are all under a similar government, and under the condition of similar laws, that is *homœonomic*.

22. The remaining question of their Essence, might consistently be answered by drawing a final conclusion from property, form, and effect, to essence, nature, and origin, which would be, that, compared with one another, they are *homœousian*.

Perhaps, for a conclusive determination of this question, further accumulation of facts may be wanted. But Schneider's hypothesis, that the ὅμοια are the remedies and the causes of disease, is very acceptable, being consistent with the facts at our command, and comporting with the doctrine of Hippocrates and Hahnemann.

And, with Newton's caution about the use of the word "forces"* it

* Philosophiae Naturalis Principia Mathematica Coloniæ Allobrogum 1760, 4° I., p. ii. ". . . . Mathematicus dundaxat est hic conceptus. Nam virium causas et sedes Physicas jam non expendo . . . . Unde caveat lector, ne per hujusmodi voces cogitet, me speciem vel modum actionis causamve at rationem Physicam alicui definire, vel centris (quae sunt puncta Mathematica) vires vere et Physice tribuere; si forte aut centra trahere, aut vires centrorum esse dixero."

might be safely said, that the ὅμοια are the forces which operate in and upon organism and remedy, representing the effects of disease and medicine upon the healthy. The *tertium comparationis* is the pathema, *i. e.* the manner in which the organism is affected by either.

23. Hahnemann, and his greatest disciples, always stoutly maintained the *hylozoic* opinion, that every thing in nature lives. The same belief is shared by the highest minds of every age, and among its adherents are Heraclitus, Anaxagoras, Aristoteles, Leibnitz, Forster, Goethe, Herbart, Ritter, Du Bois-Reymond, Draper, Moleschott, Fechner, and a host of eminent scientists of our age.

The same opinion gains new confirmation and support by the nature, properties, and efficaciousness, of our High Potencies. They, in their preparation and mutual action with the organism, prove again, what Draper states, that "there is no essential difference between the processes of organic and inorganic life, and the line of demarcation which Natural History has so far vainly attempted to define with correctness between organic and inorganic world, is merely arbitrary: either of them is reducible to motion and governed by the same laws."

24. Thus the proposed disquisition of our subject leads to the final question of the *ultimate constitution of matter*, adverted to in Joslin's prognosticon at the head of these observations.

And indeed, it would be entirely proper to inquire, what service the study of Homœopathic High Potencies might do in that direction.

Researches of that kind legitimately belong to Metaphysics. Newton's warning: "Oh, physicians, beware of metaphysics!"—was correct in his time. What then was called Metaphysics, was nominally Metaphysics, *quasi lucus a non lucendo*, whilst he himself was, in fact, the greatest metaphysician, because the greatest natural philosopher, of his age. But Metaphysics must not be understood to be mere mental philosophy and transcendentalism, but, according to Herbart's conception of it, is that branch of philosophy, the province of which is, to explain experience by philosophical conception, and which, therefore, proceeds from, and finally rests on, experience and reality. Metaphysics, says Herbart, must support Natural Philosophy and Psychology, and thereby show its accordance with itself: it must stick to facts the most certain, whilst experiments and observations multiply *in infinitum;* and experience, only, must be its ground and foundation, and no dwelling in castles of air will do instead of it.

Now, it must be owned, that we know nothing positively of the nature of health, disease, and remedy, and that their properties, and existence, are only inferred from the effects they produce in the organism. Equally so, we know nothing positively of the nature of things and forces generally, and their properties, and existence, are only inferred from the effects they produce. Hence, as Astronomy, by judging from their apparent positions, and motions, finds the true position and motion of the celestial bodies, so Metaphysics has to find the real nature and essence of things and forces from the properties and effects of things and forces, as they appear to us by correct observation.

Among these the phenomena of *Attraction* and *Repulsion*, as a general property of matter, and the *Origin of Matter by Contraries*, are problems to which our HOMŒOSIS, or the mutual action of contrary similars, is referable. Their reality, and the solution of the seeming contradiction, that contraries cooperate and, by doing so, produce thirds similar to themselves and to one another, becomes practically and scientifically explainable by the conception of *Infinitesimality of all Action.*

But this is not the place to enter, to any extent, into such metaphysical disquisitions, and a historical reminiscence must suffice.

25. The general principle of the Origin of all Matter and Motion by Contraries, was in early times conceived by Pythagoras, Heraclitus, and Anaxagoras.

The latter, moreover, distinctly taught *Simility* as a pivotal point for the constitution of matter, and also *Infinitesimality* of matter, mind and motion. And he states, especially, the origin of *affections upon the organism* to be by *Contraries*, laying down as the reason for it: "τὸ γαρ ὅμοιον 'απαθὲσ "'απὸ το̃υ 'ομοιου" i. e. because the simile is impassible from the simile. (Theophrastus Eresius.) This is a remarkable rectification of the common belief, that "*simile simili gaudet*," and, together with Hippocrates' nice observation, that "*the most contraries are not always the most contraries*," it affords a fine philosophical argument for our idea of Homœodynamicity, and medical action especially, according to which *similia similibus curantur.*

Singular, indeed, it seems, that Anaxagoras, the friend and teacher of Pericles, Euripides and Democritus, and who died when Hippocrates was thirty-two years old, and to whom belongs the merit of anatomical research prior to Aristoteles, and of whom are preserved a few most interesting views on Biology and Cosmology, and whose life, in excitement, persecution and martyrium, and in other respects, presents a parallel with that of Hahnemann; singular, we say, it is, that this early Greek philosopher should have foreshadowed, as it were, the molecular theory of our own age, and the homœomatic principle, and the Affinity of Opposition, the elemental importance of Simility and Contrariety, and the Laws of Motion, and the Infinitesimality and micrological nature of all motion and all things, and almost the Law of the Least Quantity of Action, in short, the very elements and principles of our own Homœopathic Science, which are no more nor less, than the principles of Natural Science.

Verily, as Quinctilian says, *optima veterum nova, optima novorum vetera!*

But here we take leave of the subject, resting with confidence in our hope, that Herbart's prophecy will be fulfilled: "*Much will Europe* "*learn from North America, when Philosophy shall come to blossom there.*"

CLINICAL CASES AND OBSERVATIONS.

SEVENTH SERIES.

Yet, little as it is, you see, it was of some service to him.
STERNE.

IN this final series we report some cases, where High Potencies, carried up further, and as far as the 71000th centesimally, were administered and proved successful.

These High Potencies, being of the same kind as mentioned in the Fifth Series, are prepared on a new plan, which, in proper time, will be communicated to the profession. For the present, in order to distinguish them from others, we propose to call them *Fluxion Potencies*, taking the notion from Newton's infinitesimal calculus, which assigns to the fluxion, though of infinitesimal magnitude, a finite value.

CASES.

1. VOMITUS.—M., a girl of German descent ten years old.

September 20th, 1864. On going out this morning in the street, she vomited yellow water and slime. Since then she cannot get into an erect position without vomiting again, with pain in the pit of the throat. Face pale; headache, with hot head; eyes dull; drowsy. *Bryon.* $\frac{6}{71m}$.

This relieved her promptly.

2. ASCITES.—P. a girl, American, five years old.

September 18th, 1864. Abdominal dropsy after scarlet fever. *Merc. v.* $\frac{6}{23m}$.

Removed in a short time.

3. RHEUMATISMUS.—Miss N., fourteen years old, of German descent.

May 5th, 1864. Rheumatism in the right shoulder and upper arm; painful in moving and touching it. *Bryon.* $^{2}_{71}$m. before bedtime. Next morning it was gone.

4. NEPHRITIS AND ALBUMINURIA.—Henry J., seven years old, of German descent; scrofulous; thin, delicate; black hair, gray eyes. Father died recently of inflammation of the lungs and dropsy, as they say.

September 17th, 1864. The mother says, three or four weeks ago, patient got a pustular eruption in his face, which suppurated a good deal; also, a pustule on the leg, which made quite a sore, "probably chickenpox."

Since last week his left parotid began to swell hard; but it has since decreased again. His face is, since the 13th, swollen under the eyes, where he looks quite blue; tongue coated whitish; keeps his two eyes closed all the time; no appetite except for coffee, which he wants constantly; skin hot; fever high, with headache; short breath; heart's action large and frequent. Urine last night twice, quite black; yesterday, brown sediment; now turbid, scanty, greenish, with reddish slimy sediment, 1,020 sp. g., containing much albumen. Stool yellow, lumpy, mucous; this morning quite thin. The boy is given up by his physician as beyond recovery. *Apis. mel. 42 m.* in water; teaspoonful every hour, except when sleeping.

September 18th. Fever and headache continuing; urine turbid, cloudy, somewhat greenish. *Apis m.*, 1000 in water; a teaspoonful every two hours.

September 19th. Had a very bad night. At six, P. M., terrible heat, headache, eyes closed, constant lamentation, till seven and a quarter, P.M. At twelve, A.M., some sleep; the heat unabated; pain in the right renal region, where he puts his hand on, since three, A.M. He cries already when his mother is only going to touch him, and complains much in that side on being lifted. In the forenoon less heat.

Didn't want to take medicine this morning (an unfavorable sign, always, with homœopathic patients.) Face less swollen; feet swollen over the ankles; genitals swelled. Complains still of the right renal region. Drinks not much. Kicking with hands and feet. Stool black, thin, smelling like carrion. Passed six ounces of urine in twelve hours greenish, containing much albumen, 1,020 sp. g.

Arsen., $\frac{2}{10m.}$ to be given immediately.

Arsen., $\frac{2}{600}$, at six, P. M.; and

Apis. m., $\frac{2}{20m.}$ at one o'clock in the night.

September 20th. Yesterday the heat subsided. Was very weak; could not keep his eyes open. Does not complain of his head. Stool yesterday at four, P. M., thin, brown, looking well, and without offensive odor. Slept well all night and this morning. This morning, thirst; wants water. Wanted his school things yesterday. Moaning during sleep. Yesterday passed thick urine three times; once in the night. This morning he asked for the vessel in order to pass water, for which he did not ask before. Urine brighter, somewhat turbid, without sediment, greenish; much less albumen, remarkably so; 1,020 sp. g. Very tender, with loud crying on being touched. Face sunk, eyes larger; genitals more swelled; feet swollen around the ankles and at the instep. Eight, P. M., *Arsen.*, *51 m.*

September 21st. Was quite hungry. Slept well, and had a sound stool. Face somewhat swollen; genitals much swollen, but no other swelling to be seen. Passed urine twice during the day, twice in the night, and once this morning. Urine somewhat turbid, less albuminous; 1,0225 sp.g. Eight o'clock, P. M., *Arsen. 43 m.*

September 22d. Has passed urine five times; this morning more than one pint. Genitals swollen so much, that he cannot sit straight, with stinging pain. Appetite good. Sleep and stool normal. Sings, and is quite lively. Looks better. Some perspiration at the forehead. He says, when he opens his mouth wide, he hears music. Abdomen is not swollen at all. *Arsen. 51 m.* in water; a teaspoonful once in three hours; two powders.

September 24th. Sleeps well. Had yesterday headache; the face was more swollen; the genitals were very much swollen. Ate little yesterday. Stool normal every day. Passed about a quart of urine night and morning, and some during the day. Some perspiration. Urine greenish, turbid, with less albumen; 1,0175 sp. g. *Arsen. 10 m.*, in water; a teaspoonful once in three hours; four powders.

September 27th. On the 25th he complained much of headache, with much swelling, especially on his right side, of the face, and under the eyes. Less so to-day. But the swelling of the genitals is considerable, so that the skin is shining, transparent from the distention. Yesterday, stool twice; to-day, once. Appetite good. Passed often and much urine; this morning more than ever; since then twice again. The last secretion looks much brighter, with a greenish shade; little albumen; 1,0125 sp. g. *Arsen 20 m.*, in water, a teaspoonful every three hours; six powders.

October 3d. Is quite lively. Face a little swollen about the eyes. Passes much urine, a little turbid, with little albumen. 1,010 sp. g. *Arsen. 25 m.*, in water; a teaspoonful every three hours; seven powders.

October 10th. Next day, after the last prescription, on waking up, violent headache over the eyes, so that he could not open them, lasting all day till evening; with paleness of the face, coldness, and sometimes cold sweat, icy cold head and ears. The day after, red turbid urine, like blood. Now loose cough, with choking, swallowing the expectoration down. All swelling gone. Wants now cakes and coffee, no meat. Very peevish. Passes much urine, pale, yellowish, and a little turbid; very little albumen. 1,015 sp. g. Looks very miserable. *Sulph.* $\frac{2}{55}$ *m.*

October 17th. Feels quite well. Urine slightly turbid, greenish, some albumen, on boiling colored brown, 1,025 sp. g., showing brownish granules under the microscope. *Arsen.* $\frac{5}{43}$ m.

October 24th. Urine quite clear, pale, with a slight whitish shade; no albumen; 1,015 sp. g.; face very pale, especially when sleeping; sometimes cold perspiration during sleep. *Arsen.* $\frac{5}{51}$m.

October 31st. Urine somewhat turbid, with some albumen again; 1,022 sp. g.; stool sometimes quite hard; uncovering in the night. *Merc. v.* $\frac{3}{6}$m.

November 6th. *Merc. v.* $\frac{3}{10}$m.

November 16th. Had a slimy diarrhœa the 13th. Passes much water. Urine pale yellow, with slightly turbid shade, unchanged by heat or nitric acid. Otherwise well. Wants potatoes. *Merc. v. 36 m.*

January 1st, 1865. Urinary secretions normal. Otherwise well.

OBSERVATIONS.

In medicina multa scire oportet et pauca agere.
BAGLIVI.

In conclusion, I beg to submit the following observations:

1. Homœopathic High Potencies as high as 71,000, are efficacious and curative.

2. The terminus and limit number of the efficaciousness of High Potencies is not reached yet at 71,000, and the question is still open.

3. High Potencies sometimes heal symptoms produced by lower Potencies.

4. High Potencies heal, sometimes, what lower ones did not.

5. High Potencies, as high as 71,000, are sufficient to cure by one single dose.

6. In these Higher Potencies the original substance from which they are started, is still discernible by the pathogenetic picture of the case cured, which picture is similar to the pathopoetic picture of the lower Potencies.

7. By comparing the Susceptibility of the same person in the different states of health and disease, we arrive at the possibility of finding the dose commensurate in the given case.

8. With this view, measures should be taken, to institute experiments upon certain persons all through their time of life, with regard to their ascendants and their medical history.

9. Arrangements should be made, to collect the pathematic pictures so obtained, from time to time, in one common work, forming a *Comparative Materia Medica Pura*, and running perpetually from age to age.

10. The diseases described in the allœopathic text books on Pathology, should be carefully examined into, as to their origin and complication, owing to allœopathic medication. And such observations, as are not pure and exact, should be rejected, in spite of all high authority.

11. Under treatment, frequently symptoms make their appearance, which belong to the pathopoetic action of the remedy applied, and such are acceptable as pathopoetic symptoms available for cure.

12. Pathogenetic symptoms cured by one single remedy without interference of any other remedial agent, may be considered as equivalent to pathopoetic symptoms and as available for cure.

13. The Provings and the Clinics, including the aggravations observed during treatment with High Potencies, taken together, prove, when compared, the correctness of each other.

14. The action of Homœopathic High Potencies is in no way explainable by the so-called Humoral Pathology, the quantities concerned being too fine and too little, as to be proportionable to the elements of the lymph and blood and their constituents.

15. The nervous system offers a possibility of finding a rationale for the action of Homœopathic High Potencies upon the organism.

16. Many analogies from Physiology and Pathology point to the manner in which Homœopathic High Potencies may act upon the organism.

For instance, we know, that the slightest impression upon the skin is conveyed to the brain and occasions an impression there, which is accepted to be mediated only by the nervous system. The slightest and least amount of olfactory matter is perceived by the expansion of the olfactory nerve upon the mucus membrane of the nose, and transferred to the brain, by the nerve mentioned. The least ray of light causes intolerable pain in strumous ophthalmia. In the ear of our venerable colleague, Aegidi* a flock of cotton was sufficient to prevent a train of serious perturbation of health bordering on apoplexy. The wine-taster can, on his tongue, distinguish a certain taste among different wines. Chemical changes in the bowels are perceived as pain, by the nerves distributed to them. Thoughts uttered in speech or writing by a distant individual, perhaps distant by centuries and death, enter the brain and work accordant changes, certainly not by means of the bones or muscles, but by means of the nervous system. Miasms, unapt to be isolated and so detected, affect the body and change its healthy into a morbid state, by the medium of the nervous system.

17. Physiology abounds with instances of chemical actions in the organisms modified by nervous influence. And in the face of these facts the nervous system must be considered to be the government of the Union of the organism, for its self-preservation and enjoyment, as a little Republic or Microcosm.

---

* Allg. Hom. Zeit., Vol. 65, p. 122.

18. As other agencies of similar nature, and as the so-called Imponderabilia (in reality High Potencies of Nature), Heat, Light, Electricity, Galvanism, Magnetism, Mechanical and Chemical Action, and Physical and Organical Action withal, act upon the human organism; so the Homœopathic High Potencies themselves affect the organism equally in Hygiopoesis and Pathopoesis.

19. The *modus operandi* of Homœopathic High Potencies upon the organism, cannot be more wonderful or strange than that of any other agency affecting the organism, nay, that of the contact of bodies in general.

20. This *modus operandi* depends upon the contact of the High Potencies acting upon the organism at the most conven ent point of solicitation which is found to be not the stomach, as of old, but the mucous membrane of the tongue and nose.

21. In these organs the mucous membrane, as the proper point of solicitation, presents the finest and most appropriate arrangement for taking up those fine medicinal preparations which are known by the name of Homœopathic High Potencies.

22. In this mucous membrane the terminations of the nerves in the papillæ, have not yet been discovered, and, perhaps, never will be, because the microscope can hardly attain power and clearness enough, to show the nerves, distributed in infinitesimal webs throughout the mucous membrane, in such a degree of fineness, as required for the susception of the contact of such firm substances as Homœpathic High Potencies are.

23. Nevertheless, these infinitesimal terminations of the nerves are extant, and they must be endowed by nature with forces sufficient in mutual action with the similarly infinitesimal High Potencies, to produce the physiological effect of pathopoesis and hygiopoesis.

24. This effect is conditionated and determined by the Proportionality of the Homœopathic High Potencies with the nerval terminations of the mucous membrane solicited.

25. This Proportionality is, again, determined and conditionated by the connexion of the nerve terminations with the nerve centres.

26. The action of the Homœopathic High Potencies upon the organism is the resultant of the continued equalization of mutual action between the High Potency and the nerve solicited, constituting the physiological force, hygio- or patho-poetical.

27. This action may be facilitated, or hindered, or modified, by the concurrence of the various humours and tissues of the system, standing in the relation as vehicles to the nerves.

28. Probably, all the known physical and chemical processes of Nature in infinitesimal space, are instrumental in mediating the contact between the Homœopathic High Potencies and the nerve terminations.

29. The nerve centre is that central point in relation to the peripheral nerve termination at the tongue or nose, whence and where the physiological effect of the Homœopathic High Potencies and the nerve, in

mutual action, is converted into its contrary: hygiopotic into pathopoetic action, and pathopoetic into hygiopoetic action, as the case may be:—*Metathesis Medica.*

30. This Conversion, as such, acts polarly in the opposite direction towards the periphery of the nerve centre, and there produces in a physiological order those symptoms which are known as pathopoetic or hygiopoetic symptoms respectively.

31. The pathogenetic symptoms have their centre in the nerve centre, equally so have it the hygio- and pathopoetic symptoms.

32. Therefore, the Homœopathic High Potencies, in the disease, by converting in the nerve centre the pathopoetic effect into hygiopoetic symptoms neutralize the pathogenetic effect upon the nerve centre.

33. This being done, the pathogenetic symptoms disappear, that being the effect of the hygiopoetic and pathogenetic action of the High Potencies.

34. The agencies producing the pathogenetic symptoms in the organism, are similar to the High Potencies which are known to produce similar pathopoetic symptoms.

35. The form of disease depends upon the quality of the pathogenetic High Potencies, and the form of cure depends upon that of the hygiopoetic High Potencies applied.

36. The cure with Homœopathic High Potencies, is that form of cure which is proportional to the form of disease, because the various symptoms of pathogenesis and pathopoesis are, by virtue of their Simility, proportioned to each other.

37. The natural highest aim of the organism is promoted by its self-preservation.

38. Self-preservation consists in the assimilation of nutritious matter and disassimilation of noxious matter, either matter being furnished by Potentiation of crude matter:—*Physiological Homœosis.*

39. By virtue of this assimilation the different organs grow in various degrees of organization.

40. Among them the organs, comprised under the denomination "Nervous System," show the finest organization as yet known.

41. The nervous system consists of infinitely many, immeasurable, and infinitesimal terminations of nerves, connected with comparatively few nerve centres.

42. These nerve terminations stand in specific relation to these nerve centres, and, according to this connection, act to and fro, centripetally and centrifugally, as the case may be.

43. We distinguish five different nerve centres governing the organism, interdependent among themselves, and acting according to the Law of Compensation, viz.: the mental, the motorial, the emotional, the vegetative, and the reproductive.

44. These nerve centres are interconnected, and balanced, and proportioned, so as to form, as it were, the great centre of the whole organism

as a Union, having the control of all the biological motions in all its parts.

45. All the nerve terminations being equally so interdependent, interconnected, balanced, and proportioned, by an infinitesimal network, demonstrable only by induction, as yet, lead in distinct fibres to and from the several centres.

46. But neurotic action proceeds, not only along the fibres in continual motion, but also athwart and across, independently of anatomical construction, and in all possible directions, and this dianeurotic action, apparently irregular, seems to be mediated by the nerve centres themselves as masses.

47. The nervous system presents a series of Potentiation of nervous matter, elaborated by Nature herself, from the palpable to the infinitesimal.

48. The various terms of this series are endowed with various energies, each according to its Proportionality with the other terms.

49. But the functions of the nervous system are far too little understood as yet, as to allow a conclusive inference as to the *modus operandi.*

50. In this respect, it is almost hopeless, to get any satisfactory result, because it seems to be impossible, to get between the mutual action of bodies. For, you are not between the mutual action of two bodies approaching each other for contact, when you stand between them and feel their impact upon you. For, then, even the mutual action takes place between you and the impinging body on either side.

51. Only from the result, we can judge, what may have occurred; but we can never enter the circuit itself which every mutual action, according to its own nature, accomplishes apart of ourselves.

52. And this is all we can fairly expect to know, and we must be satisfied with making observations from the facts before us, and drawing correct conclusions therefrom.

53. Consequently, it is altogether improper, to call for an explanation of the *modus operandi* of the action of Homœopathic High Potencies upon the organism, without previously explaining the *modus operandi* of the origin of disease or pathogenesis, as the action of the unknown pathogenetic High Potencies upon the organism.

54. Hence, it would be unreasonable, to doubt, or reject, Homœopathy on the ground of the difficulty in explaining the *modus operandi* of infinitesimal remedies. The difficulty is the same with the *modus operandi* of any other remedy or agency.

55. Those who press this difficulty, using it as a weapon against Homœopathy, only forget, or mask, or disguise, their own ignorance, and their inability to prove themselves, what they blame us for not proving. If they will explain to us the *modus operandi* of any medicine and of life in general, we will explain to them the *modus operandi* of Homœopathic High Potencies.

56. The distinct and clear action of Homœopathic High Potencies upon

the organism, is an established fact. From it, by careful investigations, to be continued through many ages, we may, by and by, be enabled to deduce the action of the nervous system in its minutest details, which now escape the knife of the anatomist, the lens of the microscopist, the reagent of the chemist and the astatic needle of the physicist. (See Vogt. Physiol. Briefe, 1856, 2d ed. Vol. I. p. 251, 309.)

57. An exact Science falls short of its duty, if it admits, or acknowledges, only that which crosses the field of vision of its own special sense. To be exact, it must include, necessarily, the philosophical and mathematical deductions from facts and observations, as well as the acquirements of other exact Sciences.

58. The present defects, insufficiency, inability, and incomprehension of Physiology, however, does not materially interfere with the practical Art of Healing itself. Since Hahnemann's great revelation, the want of theory has ceased to furnish to Medicine an excuse for not curing what proves to be curable, with or without a theory. Fact is, that in what is called disease, the only reality positively observable and discernible, is the totality of the symptoms, that is, the physiological sum of the phenomena observed. And the fact is, that the *Symptom-Simility*, experimentally discovered, and firmly established, is, under the *Law of Proportionality*, a safe guide for the cure of the disease, that is of the patients, by *Potencies*, low and high. *Similia Similibus* CURANTUR!

APPENDIX.

APPENDIX.

I.

THE HOMŒOPATHIC DOSE IS INFINITESIMAL.

A HISTORICAL ARGUMENT.

In certis unitas, in dubiis libertas, in omnibus charitas.
AUGUSTINUS.

Homœopathic is that which pertains or belongs to Homœopathy. To know, then, what is homœopathic, we must know, what is Homœopathy. Homœopathy is a matter of fact and a historical reality. It is the Art of Healing established and named by Hahnemann, and history knows no other Homœopathic Art of Healing, but that founded by Hahnemann.

The Dose is the quantity of medicine administered to the patient. To know, then, what the Homœopathic Dose is, we must know, what dose that is, which history shows to be peculiar to Homœopathy. And this is the dose originally employed and taught by Hahnemann as the dose properly belonging to the Homœopathic Art of Healing.

Apart from theory and philosophy, opinion, and estimation, the sure and safe way of finding, what the Homœopathic Dose is, appears to be the natural way of historical inquiry, to know the facts in history, showing the origin, nature, and development, of Homœopathy, and of its Posology and Dose in particular.

These facts are known to history. They are recorded in the writings of the founder of Homœopathy, such as are published and before the world, ever since 1795. His statements are the evidence of facts, and they are the very best kind of evidence, authentic and documentary.

On a close examination of Hahnemann's writings, with a single eye to the purpose of ascertaining these facts, we discover, that the original and true text of them is sometimes different from the translations of it. This is remarkably so in all matters relating to the Homœopathic Dose. As an instance we refer to the Organon, the standard-work and text-book on Homœopathics. We have before us the English translation by Stratten, republished by Radde, and commonly received, in this country. Comparing this with the German original, we are astonished to find, that this English translation not only is, indeed, what Stratten calls it in the preface, a version, rather than a translation, but also, that especially in all matters relating to the Dose, it is defective, inaccurate, sometimes decidedly untrue, not to say falsifying the record.

Since, from this, it may be naturally supposed, that those of our profession, as well as our opponents, who derive their knowledge of Homœopathy from translations, are easily misled and deceived as to the truth in the matter; we have, in the following pages, endeavored to give a correct and faithful translation of the principal passages in Hahnemann's works, including the Organon, relating to the Dose, with a view of rendering the true meaning of the words as literally as possible, at the same time avoiding paraphrase, and religiously preserving the quaint, complicated, square-rigged, elaborate, latin-like style of the author, which to the general reader appears somewhat stiff and unwieldy, but to the careful student and scholar offers the never ending delight of entering into the spirit of a great genius and benefactor. It is the Organon, especially, which gains and grows upon you, the more you study it, and the more your faculties, by its study, develop and increase and expand into a clear comprehension of it. The observation of this fact, by experience, led our Bœnninghausen, to inculcate upon the profession, his advice, to iterate and reiterate the diligent perusal and assiduous study of this work, as the fountain-head of our knowledge of Homœopathics.

To come to our historical argument, we have to premise a word or two, as to the reason for presenting it. This is the circumstance, that the second generation of Homœopathicians, and many of our brethren at the present time, in their conception of Homœopathy are discriminating between Homœopathy and Hahnemann, and separating the element of Simility from the element of Infinitesimality. By a curious mistake, for which reasons are obvious and here not to be adverted to in particular, they attempt to emancipate Homœopathy from Hahnemann. Unguardedly confounding fact and theory, they undertake to eliminate the Homœopathic Dose from Homœopathy, and openly express their belief, that the question of the Dose is not fundamental for Homœopathy.

This is not only inconsistent with historical truth, as will be shown presently, but it is also a logical error, in as much as it is an attempt, in a real thing and in its practical application, to separate and keep separate, that which is by nature inseparably united in it, viz.: Quality and Quantity. It is like severing a man's body from his soul, and then insisting, that he is a live man.

There is, in fact, no thing in the world, which has not its quality *and* quantity at the same time and together. In cogitation they may be considered separately; but that is only a psychological process. In reality, in the thing, as it exists, and as it is used, there is always its quantity together with its quality. Without the one or the other, it would not be a real thing, and not be the identical thing, nor could it be used at all.

The same is the case with Homœopathy, as a historical reality. Simility relates to the quality of disease and remedy, and Infinitesimality relates to the quantity of the same. A homœopathic remedy is unconceiveable and impracticable without uniting its quantity with its quality, and, historically, it never existed without so uniting both. Its Posology has ever been as homœopathical as its Materia Medica.

The quality is not disputed. All concede it to be fundamental, and even the dominant school seem to tire out of attacking Homœopathy on account of the Simile.

But as to the quantity, there is much doubting, wrangling, and barking, all around. Being so little, it is the subject of so much controversy; being so much ridiculed, it is so much dreaded and avoided; and it being impossible to be kept out, it is treated as an open question.

Now, as to the quantity, the fact is, that we do not know, what quantity it is, which gives us the symptoms in the natural disease; but we do know, what quantity it is which gives us the symptoms in artificial disease (by our Provings), and we do know, what quantity it is, which effects the cure (by our Clinics). In the given case we know positively, and distinctly, that it is such and such a quantity of a medicine, given to the healthy, which has produced or cured a given set of symptoms. And, since the quality of a medicine which makes it a certain definite substance, such as Aconite, Gold, Silver, etc., can not be severed, in use, from its quantity, because it cannot be administered otherwise, than in a certain definite quantity: the conclusion is unavoidable, that it is the quantity as well as the quality of a medicine which makes it a remedy, and is instrumental in the production or removal of the symptoms observed after its administration. This is self-evident, but most clearly transparent in the fact, that certain substances, (*e. g.*, Opium,) which in great quantity act poisonous, are comparatively inert in little quantity, and that, on the other hand, certain substances, (*e. g.*, Sepia,) which in large doses are indifferent, are in small doses exerting a poisonous action, making seriously sick.

Quantity, then, is indispensable for the action of any medicine of any quality; but it is mostly so for the action of the homœopathic quality, which is the only remedial quality, recognized by us all.

The homœopathic quantity is that which is just sufficient to overcome the disease, and the least of it is sufficient, and hence the least possible or infinitesimal of it is homœopathical.

Whilst the Simility of the symptoms represents that quality of the disease which we observe as the effect of the Quiddity, as it were, of the known or unknown substance, or agent, acting upon the organism; the Infinitesimality represents the quantity of the same, the substratum, as it were, of the phenomena, rendered accessible to us by means of the Simility.

Now, Higher Analysis shows, that Quantity is something extending in a series of all possible and practicable quantities, from the measureable to the immeasureable, from the ponderable to the imponderable, from the numerable to the innumerable, from the crudest to the finest, from the greatest to the least. And this is the Infinite Series of Magnitude.

Therefore, as in any reality, so in Homœopathy, it is logically impossible to separate Quantity from Quality, Infinitesimality from Simility.

Also, physically considered, this inseparability of the two elements of Homœopathy, the entirety of Homœopathy, the intimate union of both the quantitative and qualitative elements, Infinitesimality and Simility, in the one whole of Homœopathy, is a fact natural, real, existent and established.

Infinitesimal means infinitely little, and no fact is so certain as this, that all bodies, including the human organism, consist of infinitesimal parts; and especially the Higher Analysis, introduced by Homœopathic Potentiation, together with the experience had, furnishes positive and conclusive proof of the Infinitesimality of all matter and action. This is not to be gainsayed any more. It is no use theorizing or quibbling about it. Dialectics will never disprove a fact. And as a fact, beyond all Transcendentalism, Moralism, Dogmatism and Mysticism, it stands proved and incontrovertible, that bodies do consist of infinitesimal parts. Only, the difficulty is to assign them, being so diminutive as to escape perception so easily, that the superficial observer would fain to believe them apparent nothings, whilst the careful observer, arriving at a point anticipated to be final, only discovers the beginning of a new series of infinitely many links of quantities. Thus the astronomer, the more he magnifies his telescopic power, the more he sees of the unseen, and, behind all the presupposed nothing, perceives to be an infinitude of worlds.

It is clear enough, then, that the crude substance of any remedy of ours, consists of Infinitesimals. If any one doubts it, let him count and measure the number and volume of particles of one grain of Arsenic or of one of the precipitated metals in dust-form! Or let him try it with fluids. There the infinitesimal particles run together in liquid form, so that with our senses we perceive only the assemblage or aggregation of Infinitesimals, and not the Infinitesimals themselves.

But still, the Infinitesimals are there, and make the thing, and do the work. And the same applies to our remedial substance.

But, you ask, how many Infinitesimals do you want for a cure? "As many as sufficient, just enough, and no more." This is the plain, straightforward answer, given by Hahnemann. Sufficient to cure, is all, that is necessary to cure. The sufficient quantity is the curative quantity; the *least* of it, if a Simile, is a curative quantity and is sufficient; and, hence, the least of it, is all which is required for the Dose; and that is an infinitesimal quantity of it. Here you have the answer to your question, and with it the very principle of the Homœopathic Dose.

Thus much as to the logic and philosophy of those who insist upon disconnecting Infinitesimality from Simility. But considering their proposition in the light of history, it must be said, that it is inconsistent with truth to contend, as they do, that the infinitesimal dose is indifferent and not fundamental for Homœopathy. History disproves and confutes their assumtion altogether.

For, from the first to the last, in the history of the life of Homœopathy, given to it by Hahnemann, we find it to be the fact, that the minimal dose of the Simile is established to be sufficient for the cure, and that the most possible littleness and fineness of the dose is invariably presented, and urged, as the constant *proviso* for the practical application of the remedy.

This is historically the Posology of Homœopathy. As a matter of fact, the minimal, *i. e.*, infinitesimal, dose was never, at any time, separate from Homœopathy; on the contrary, from the beginning, it was its inherent nature and characteristic; and on the same principle, and in the same direction, it was constantly, and continually, followed up, and developed, by Hahnemann himself, and by wholesouled Homœopathicians after him.

This is proved, as we mentioned before, by Hahnemann's own statements.

It would take too much space to reproduce all the passages of his works relating to the Dose. But it is certain, that none of them is conflicting with the others. They are all of the same even tenor, they all evidence the fact, that from the start, from the moment of the very conception of Homœopathy, he never mentions the homœopathical remedy without providing at the same time for the *little dose*, *the minimal dose*, *and the least possible dose of it*, AS THE HOMŒOPATHIC DOSE. Always in his statements, the quantity of the dose is inseparably connected with the quality of the remedy; always the prescription of Simile is united with the proviso of the Minimum Dose. This is so, not only in the writings of his higher age, as some believe, but from beginning to end.

Commencing with Hahnemann's discovery or creation of Homœopathy, and continuing with the most distinct and striking passages, here presented, of his works, mainly of the Organon, we feel confident, that the closest scrutiny of these statements will leave not the least doubt of the fact, that the father and educator of Homœopathy, from the first and throughout, stated, and insisted, that the least dose of the Simile is sufficient to cure, and that he always made it the characteristic and indispensable condition of the Homœopathic Art of Healing, that the Homœopathic Dose should be little, only just great enough to overcome the disease, and no more; that it should be a minimal dose, as little as possible, and as fine as possible; impressing it upon the mind, that almost never it could be given little enough and must be infinitely little, that is, infinitesimal. Nay, it is historically demonstrable, that the very thing which gave him the first impulse towards the conception of Homœopathy, was the very question of the Dose. And in this sense, and in point of time too, it may be truly said, that Microdosia is the very condition precedent of Homœopathy itself.

Singularly enough, it is taken for granted, that the cure by Symptom-Simility forms the only new and highest merit of the great man we speak of, and yet, to do so, is raising a trivial question of priority, without occasion for it, and without necessity for Homœopathy. And it is almost injustice to those physicians who, as Hahnemann alleges himself, previous to him, occasionally touched upon, and unconsciously followed, the same idea of Simility as Principle of Cure. And it is belittling Hahnemann himself, not to vote him the crown for that which is beyond controversy new and greatest in him, namely, his Potentiation, which we do not hesitate, to declare, to be the greatest discovery of the age, reaching far beyond Medicine into the realms of Natural Science.

None of those before Hahnemann had ever touched or appreciated the Infinitesimality of Dose, nor had any of them ever connected it with the Simility of Symptoms. Hahnemann, first of all, and alone, saw and discovered and practically applied to Medicine the Minimal Dose ; he, first and alone, in Medicine realized the truth and importance of the great Economical Law of Nature which we call the Law of the Least Quantity of Action. His, and nobody else's, is the merit of first having carried the same into execution, by his own discovery of Potentiation, as the means of lessening, refining, and infinitesimalizing the remedy, thereby rendering the dose as homœopathical as the remedy is, and thus establishing the practical usefulness and scientific preeminence of Homœopathic Medicine above all others.

This discovery is, indisputably, Hahnemann's own. It caused wonderment at first. Few understood it. Few dared to countenance a thing seemingly so extravagant. Derision was easy and cheap. But it survived all that. By dint of firmness, caution, and perseverance, by laborious experiment, and careful observation, it was secured. And now it begins to be recognized as one of the great features of Homœopathy.

Already, the *usus loquendi*, and the forerunners and popularizers of Science, general literature, periodicals, and public opinion, have adopted the term "homœopathical" as synonymous and identical with minimal, extremely fine, atomic, corpuscular, molecular, unassignable, infinitely little and infinitesimal. And in spite of all opposition, general attention is riveted to the subject. Experience is increasing, and facts are accumulating, and thus, before long, we may trust to see the matter thoroughly sifted and the whole truth elicited. The stone which the builders rejected, is becoming the head of the corner.

The sunbeam of this discovery of Potentiation, long shut out, is, from day to day, spreading more and more, and in the flood of light, coming from it and illuminating the ages to come, the imposing form of Hahnemann, the discoverer, will stand out in bold relief against the sky. The opposition to the Simile was never as violent, and persistent, as it was to the Minimum, and it is dying out like that to the Simplex. But the wildest torrent of abuse was always directed against the Minimum. The higher, then, will be the glory, the greater the triumph of Hahnemann and Homœopathy, when, with the full understanding of both, the Minimum shall be revindicated.

In 1789, Hahnemann was sick of the practice of Medicine. "After discovering the weakness and mistakes of my teachers and of my books," he says, "I fell into a state of melancholical indignation, which almost "created a complete disgust against the study of Medicine. I was on "the point to believe, that the whole art is null and void and incapable of "any improvement. I gave myself up to my lonesome meditations, and "concluded to set no limit to my considerations, until I should have "arrived at the decisive resolution." (Aesculap in der Wagschale in Kleine medic. Schriften, ed. Stapf, Dresd. & Leipz. Arnold, 1829, Vol. II., p. 247.)

At that time, he made his celebrated investigations in Pharmacy and Chemistry, and translated many works in relation to the auxiliary sciences of Medicine, enriching them with many valuable annotations.

Whilst translating the Materia Medica of Cullen in 1790, he became disgusted with the labored theoretical explanation of the antipyretic power of the Peruvian bark, which Cullen had given, and he resolved on taking half an ounce of the drug himself, for the purpose of finding out the rationale of its power in suppressing the intermittent fever. A chill similar to this miasmatic fever followed, and led him to the observation, that it is the Simility of the symptoms which constitutes the curative power of the bark.

In 1796, six years later, for the first time in public, he announced his new principle: *Similia Similibus*, and dilated upon it as follows:

"You need only know, on the one side the diseases of the human "body exactly according to their essential character and their casualties, "and on the other side the pure effects of the remedies, i. e. the essential "character of the specific artificial disease, usually excited by them, "together with the casual symptoms originating *from the difference of "the dose*, the form, etc., and when selecting for the natural given disease "a remedy producing a *most possibly similar* artificial disease, you will "be able to cure the hardest diseases." (Versuch ueber ein neues Princip zur Auffindung der Heilkræfte der Arzneisubstanzen, etc., in Kl. Schr. Vol. I., p. 154.)

"The *most possibly similar*," he says: that is. similar in *quantity* as well as in *quality*, because he puts the symptoms from the dose *together* with the symptoms from the disease! And even in this early exposition we recognize the acknowledged value of subjective symptoms which are, most characteristically, elicited by fine doses.

No less distinct, and to the point, in regard to the fineness of Dose, is the note which is affixed to the sentence above quoted.

"If we mean to go to work *little by little*, as the cautious physician "should do, we give this ordinary remedy ONLY *in such a dose*, as to "*almost imperceptibly* show the artificial disease to be expected from it, "(it still acts after all by virtue of its tendency to excite such an artificial "disease,) and go up in the Dose by degrees as to be certain, that the "intended internal change of the bodily system ensues forcefully enough, "although with manifestations *in violence far behind* the natural symp-

"toms of disease. Thus we shall cure gently and surely. But, if we "want to act rapidly, provided only, that the remedy be properly and "well chosen, we shall also certainly attain our object, though with "some danger of life, and effect what amongst peasants is sometimes "roughly done by empyricists, and what they call a miraculous cure or a "horse-cure—curing a disease lasting for years, in a few days; an under-"taking which proves the correctness of my principle, indeed, but at the "same time the foolhardiness of the operator."

In the same Article (p. 155) he says: "a somewhat large dose of "Hyoscyamus-juice often leaves behind, as after-action, a great timidity. "*A little dose* of opium gives specific and almost instantaneous relief."

Further on, (p. 157) speaking of a dose of Chamomilla, two drops and a half of the ethereal oil, he continues: "The dose was much *too strong* "for her. By this it explains itself, why Cham. is found to be so helpful "in after-pains, in too great a mobility of the fibre, and in hysteria, IF "employed in *doses* in which it can not itself *perceptibly* excite *the like* "(therefore *in far lesser ones*, than the one mentioned)."

And, speaking of Arnica-root, (p. 159) he says: "here, in order to "become helpful, in diarrhœas without pus, it must be administered "ONLY *in so little doses*, that it does not manifestly purge" ..... "From the abuse of an infusion of Arnica-flowers I saw glandular swell-"ings arise. I should err very much, if with *more moderate doses* it "would not cure similar swellings." .... Several instances of curing by "moderate doses," what was produced by "stronger doses" of the same substances, are given.

From a passage in an Article, published in 1797, in Hufeland's Journal (Sind die Hindernisse der Gewissheit und Einfachheit der praktischen Arzneikunde unuebersteiglich? Kl. Schr. Vol. I., p. 16,) it appears, that Hahnemann, several years before, had cured with simple remedies, and single doses. "May I confess it, that for several years since, I never "administered anything else, but one single remedy at a time, and at "once, and that I have never repeated it, until the action of the former "dose had expired? ... May I confess, that I was successful in this "manner, and that I have cured to the satisfaction of my patients, and "that I have seen things which I could not have seen otherwise?"

In 1799, (p. 227,) in an Article on the cure and prophylaxis of Scarlet-fever, he says: "the burning heat, the sleepy stupor, the agonizing "jactitation, with vomiting, diarrhœa, also accompanied with convul-"sions, in a very short time (at the most in an hour) was removed by *a* "*very little quantity* of opium," either externally on a *bit of paper* (according to the size of the child, of a half or one inch wide and long,) "moistened with strong opium-tincture, and left laying on the pit of the "stomach, until it dried up.

"NOTE. With little and other children who will not keep still so "long, the paper is kept about a minute's time."

"For external application, I used a tincture of one part of *finely pow-*

"*dered* crude opium, *dissolved in twenty parts of thin alcohol* within a "week at a cool place, shaking it at times."

"For internal use I had *one drop* of this tincture *intimately mixed with* "*five hundred drops* of strongly *watered* alcohol, and of this mixture *one* "*drop*, carefully shaken through *with five hundred drops* of again strongly "*watered* alcohol. Of this rarified opium-tincture (containing in each "drop *one five millionth part of a grain* of opium,) *one drop* for a four- "years child, and *two drops* for a ten-years child, was superabundantly "*sufficient* to extinguish that state."

(p. 228.) "NOTE. In *what little dose* the medicaments acting upon "the whole system of the animated parts, if in the right place, *do accom-* "*plish their object*, is incredible, at least incredible to those of my fellow "artists who believe to be compelled, to treat suckling children by half- "grain doses of the extract of Opium, and who possess skill enough, to "charge a multitude of other causes with the often rapid asphyxia."

(p. 232.) "I gave to this ten-years old girl, already affected with the "first symptoms of Scarlet-fever, a dose of this plant"—Belladonna—($\frac{1}{432000}$ *part of a grain* of the dried juice.)

"NOTE. A dose *all too large* for this age, at least if given for pro- "phylactic purposes, but probably *just adequate* for the symptoms of "Scarlet-fever already so far progressed, which, however, I know not "positively. Therefore, I *cannot advise* an unqualified imitation of this "case, still not dissuade, since the Scarlet-fever is an infinitely greater "evil, than some unpleasant affections from a *somewhat strong* dose of "Belladonna."

(p. 234.) Prescription for potentiating Belladonna for prophylaxis ($\frac{1}{24000000}$ *part of a grain* of dried juice in each drop,) *one dose* to be given once in seventy-two hours.

(p. 239.) Likewise: Chamomilla $\frac{1}{800000}$ *part of a grain* of dried juice, in a drop, to be given once a day.

1801. (p. 240 from Hufeland's Journal: Ueber die Kraft kleiner Gaben der Arzneien, etc.,) "You ask me urgently; 'what, then, $\frac{1}{100000}$ "part of a grain of Belladonna can effect?' The word 'can' is offen- "sive to me. Let us not ask the compendia, but let us ask nature: what "*does* $\frac{1}{100000}$ part of a grain of Belladonna effect? Even the healthiest "robust thrasher will be affected with the most violent and dangerous "symptoms, if this grain, by trituration, is accurately dissolved in much "water (f. i. two pounds), if their mixtion is made very thoroughly, by "shaking it in a bottle for five minutes, and if he is taking it by spoon- "fuls within six or eight hours. These two pounds contain about ten "thousand drops. If, now, one of these drops is mixed again with two "thousand drops (six ounces) of water, under strong shaking, *one tea-* "*spoonful of that mixture* (about twenty drops of it), when given every "two hours, will cause in a similarly strong man not much less violent "symptoms, if he is sick. Such a dose amounts to about *one millionth* "*part of a grain*. He will, I say, come near the edge of the grave, from "several teaspoonfuls of this mixture, *if* he was fully sick before, and "*if* his sickness was of that kind, that Belladonna was adapted to it."

"Infinitely different it is with the *solution*, and especially with the "*intimate solution*. This may be *as thin as you please;* it touches, in its "passage into the stomach, still more points of the living fibre, and "because the medicament acts not atomically, but only dynamically, "excites *far stronger symptoms* than the compact pill can do, which con- "tains a million times more parts of medicine (remaining inactive.)"

(p. 243.) "Will it, at last, be learned to be understood, *how little*, *how* "INFINITELY LITTLE" [infinitesimal] "the doses need be in the sick "state, in order to affect the body strongly? Yes! they affect it strongly, "when chosen wrongly; . . . . they affect it *just as strongly*, if chosen "right. The greatest disease often yields in a few hours."

"The more the disease approximates to an acute one, *the lesser doses* of "medicaments (I mean of the best selected) it requires, in order to dis- "appear. Also, the chronic diseases connected with debility and general "distemper require *no greater doses*" . . . .

(p. 244.) "He who is satisfied with those general hints, will also "believe me, when I assure him, that I removed several paralyses by the "use, during several weeks, of a *very rarefied* Belladonna solution, where "the whole cure did *not require a full one hundred thousandth part of a* "*grain* of dried Belladonna juice, and some periodical nervous diseases, "dispositions to furuncles, etc., required *not quite one millionth part* for "the whole cure."

1805 (Heilkunde der Erfahrung Kl. Schr. Vol. II. p. 21.) "NOTE. A "medicine which, given to a healthy man, simple and unmixed, in suita- "bly large dose, brings about a distinct effect, a distinct series of peculiar "symptoms, retains the *tendency* of exciting the like, *even in the* LEAST "DOSE."

(p. 26.) "Equally worthy of admiration is the truth, that there is *no* "medicament which, curatively applied, would be *weaker* than the dis- "ease to which it is adequate—no disease-stimulus, to which the positive "and most possibly analogous medicine-stimulus would not be *superior*.

"If not only the correct (positive) remedy is selected, BUT ALSO THE "DOSE rightly hit (*incredibly little doses are sufficient for the curative pur-* "*pose*) the remedy effects . . . ."

"In this case" [after the homœopathic aggravation during the first hour after taking the first dose] "the cure of an acute disease is usually "finished *by the first dose*.

"But, when the first dose of the fully adequate curative remedy was "not somewhat greater than the disease, and hence nothing followed "of that peculiar aggravation in the first hour; then, still, the disease is "extinguished to the greatest part, and only *few always* LESSER DOSES are "required to annihilate it entirely."

"If here *always lesser doses* would not be given, but equally great or "greater ones, then, (after the now already disappeared original disease) "arise mere medicine symptoms, a kind of an artificial unnecessary "disease."

(p. 35.) "Neither must it be believed, that this *noxiousness of excessive "doses* belongs only to the (curative) remedies positively applied. The "palliatives expose to equally great injuries by *excess of their doses;* for "medicaments are per se noxious substances which *only in the commen- "surate dose* become remedies by adaptation of their natural pathopoetic "force to the disease analogous to it (positively or negatively)."

(p. 36.) Treatment of a girl excessively heated from dancing, with some hot tea, containing a small quantity of spirits, instead of giving cold water, or ice, in large quantities.

"NOTE. This latter example at the same time shows the correctness of "the *position*, that, when the state of disease is in the extremest degree "and only a few hours remain for the cure, then the application of the "positive (curative) remedies IN VERY LITTLE DOSES is infinitely prefer- "able to that application of the palliatives, even if they should at first be "given *in very little quantity.* Even if the latter should not do any harm, "it is, at least, certain, that it helps nothing, whilst THE LEAST DOSE of "the well adapted curative remedy can save from death, if only a few "hours remain for the cure." . . . .

(p. 37.) "But, how much the sensitiveness to medicine-stimuli of the "body is heightened, of that only the exact observer has an idea. It "transcends all belief, when the disease has reached a high degree. A "senseless, prostrated, comatose Typhus patient, deaf against all shaking "and shouting, is speedily brought to consciousness BY THE LEAST DOSE "of Opium, even if it should be *millions of times less than ever prescribed* "by any mortal."

"The sensitiveness to medicine-stimuli of the highly diseased body, "rises in many cases to such a degree, that potencies begin to act upon "and excite it, of which the existence even has been denied, because "they show no effect, upon the healthy firm body, and in several diseases "not appropriate for them."

He, then, alludes to Animalism (Animal Magnetism) as follows:

"This animal force does not show itself, at all, between two robust, "healthy persons, *not because it were nothing*, but because it is much *too "little*, as to become, under the wise intentions of God, perceptible be- "tween healthy persons, whilst the same influence (entirely impercep- "tible in the transition from healthy upon healthy) frequently acts only "more than too violently in those states of morbid sensitiveness and "mobility, just as *very little doses* of other curative medicines in a very "diseased body."

The same he states as to the magnet and contact of metals.

(p. 38.) "On the other hand it is as true as worthy of astonishment, "that even the robustest persons, being affected with chronic diseases, "notwithstanding their general bodily strength, and notwithstanding "their bearing with impunity even noxious stimuli of various kind in "great quantity (overloadings with food and spirituous drinks, purga-"tives, etc.); yet, as soon as the medicine positively helpful for this "chronic evil, is administered to them, experience from the LEAST POS-"SIBLE *dose* just as full an impression as if they were suckling babes."

(p. 39.) "This dynamical action of the medicines, like the vitality "itself, by which it is reflected upon the organism, is *almost purely* "*spiritual*, most strikingly so that of the remedies used positively "(curatively), with the *singular peculiarity*, that the all too strong dose "may injure and cause considerable disorder in the body, but *a little dose* "even THE LEAST POSSIBLE, cannot be unhelpful, if only the remedy is "indicated."

(p. 43.) "To produce the most beneficial effects, always a sole remedy "is fit, wholly without admixture, IF it only is the best chosen, *the most* "*adequate* IN THE RIGHT DOSE."

(p. 46.) "I have already said, that the *least possible dose* of a positively "acting medicine is already *sufficient* for the *full* effect."

In the same year, 1805, appeared the *Fragmenta de viribus medicamentorum positivis, sive in sane corpore humano observatis* Lips. Barth., where, in the preface, p. 3, he urges the littleness of the dose "(VEL PARVA QUANTITATE *ingesta.*)"

1809. (Belehrung uber das herrschende Fieber, from the Deutsch. Allg. Anzeiger, in Kl. Schr. Vol. II., p. 86.)

"The seed which is capable of producing these symptoms (Nux vom.) "*is*, among all known vegetable medicines, the only one which is capa-"ble of curing a great part of these prevailing fevers within a short time, "but ONLY THUS, that a *very little dose* is given of it, at first every four, "afterwards only every six days."

"*The least atom of it in powder*,, or *very little only of a solution*, every "drop of which contains a trillionth of a grain of this seed, is FULLY "SUFFICIENT *for the dose*, and commensurable to the intention * * *"

(p. 87.) "How can these *high potential* medical-substances help it, "that their doses, weighed after our clumsy medicinal weights by drams, "scruples and grains, are yet *much too large* for healing purposes?"

(p. 88.) "But now, if only one-tenth part of a grain of this mineral "(Arsen. alb.) was often found to be dangerous, that is, in other words, "all too powerful, what did prevent the physicians, if they only would "have thought it over a little, to try whether a thousandth or a millionth "of a fraction of a grain, or *a lesser yet*, becomes a *moderate dose*, and, if "so little a fraction of a grain would have been found to be still too "clumsy a dose of this most highpotential of all remedies (which it is "indeed),—what did prevent them, from *lessening the fraction much* "*farther yet*, until they would have seen, that *a sixtillionth of a grain in* "*solution* becomes to be a mild and STILL FULLY SUFFICIENTLY POWER-"FUL (in our case SPECIFICALLY CURATIVE) DOSE,—being administered "once every 5—10 days" * * *

This brings us up to the year 1810, when the Organon was first published, which has had five editions up to the year 1833. In none of these editions anything is to be found, as to the Dose, not contained in the last edition.

In those intervening years Hahnemann steadily advanced, true to his original views of the Infinitesimality of the Homœopathic Dose. Thus in his celebrated Dissertation "de Helleborismo Veterum" in 1812, where he asserted the littleness and fineness of Dose into the very teeth of the Leipzig Faculty ("*minuta pulveris subtilioris dosis*"—"*minima dosis*"); and in his Articles "On the mode of Healing the prevailing nervous or hospital fever" in 1814, and "On the Uncharitableness to suicides" in 1819; and in his Petition to Government "On the self-preparing and self-dispensating of medicaments on the part of the homœopathic physicians," in 1820, and so on.

The latter document, the Petition to Government, contains some striking passages on our subject, which cannot be omitted, being of great historical value.

(Kl. Schr. Vol. II., p. 195.) "According to this more perfected mode "of healing, I require for the cure, even of the greatest diseases, hitherto "deemed incurable, *only finest possible doses* of simple substances, partly "of solutions in mere alcohol of some minerals and several metals, with-"out assistance of any acid, (preparations known only to me, but to no "chemistry, consequently to no apothecary), partly *equally fine doses* of "vegetable and animal substances,—always *only one dose of a single* "*simple remedy—doses which are so little*, that, in the usual unmedicinal "vehicle (sugar of milk), they are *entirely imperceptible by means of the* "*senses and all cogitable analysis of Chemistry.*"

"This *ineffable littleness of doses* of simple medicinal substances, in this "new art of healing, removes all possible suspicion of a noxious greatness "of the dose of simple medicine, which is given to the sick."

(p. 197.) "And yet this *uncommon fineness of doses* of all dynamically "acting medicines, is *unavoidably necessary in this new art*, so excellent "for the purpose of healing every disease, but *indispensable for the cure* "of the chronic diseases, hitherto abandoned as incurable."

(p. 199.) "I HOLD NONE TO BE MY FOLLOWER, who, besides an irre-"proachable truly moral conduct, does NOT exercise the new art AT LEAST "IN SUCH A MANNER, that his remedy given to the patient contains in an "unmedicinal vehicle (sugar of milk or watered alcohol) the medicine "*in such a little fine dose*, that neither the senses, nor chemical analysis "could discover in it the least absolutely injurious medicament, even not "at all the least properly medicinal thing; all of which presupposes *a* "*littleness of dose* which, beyond contradiction, makes all apprehension "of every medical state-superintendence disappear."

From 1811—1821, the first edition of the "Materia Medica Pura" appeared in print.

In 1828, the first edition of the "Chronic Diseases" followed.

In 1833, Hahnemann published the fifth, and last, edition of the Organon, which we may consider as the exposition of his ripest intellect, up to that time.

We select the following passages as some most positive statements of the fact, which is here proved historically.

(Organon der Heilkunst, Fifth edition, Dresd. & Leipz. Arnold 1833. Preface p. VII.) "Homœopathics, therefore, avoids even the least "weakening, also, as much as possible, every excitation of pain, because "pain also takes away the strength, and therefore, it uses for the cure "ONLY such medicines, the effects of which in changing and altering "(dynamically) the disposition, it knows exactly, and then it seeks out "such a one, the forces of which, changing the disposition, (their medic- "inal disease) is able to lift the present natural disease by Simility. "(*Similia Similibus*), and it gives to the patient the same *singly, but in* "RARE *and* FINE DOSES (SO LITTLE, *that without causing pain and weak- "ening, they just suffice, to lift the natural evil by means of the reacting "energy, of the vital force*) with the success, that, without in the least "weakening, tormenting, or plagueing him, the natural disease is extin- "guished, and the patient, already during the amelioration, soon gains "in strength of itself, and thus is cured."

(p. 78.) "§ 25. But *now*, the only and infallible oracle of the healing "art, the pure experience, teaches in all careful experiments, that really "THAT MEDICINE which in its action upon healthy human bodies has "proved itself able to beget the most symptoms in Simility, to be found "in the case of disease which is to be cured, *does*, IN DULY POTENTIATED "AND LESSENED DOSES, speedily, radically, and lastingly, abolish and "convert into health, the totality of the symptoms of this state of dis- "ease, that is, the whole present disease."

(p. 94.) "§ 26. This RESTS upon that *Homœopathic Law of Nature*, "though not unforboded, but hitherto not recognized, which lies forever "at the bottom of all true healing:

"A WEAKER *dynamic affection is in the living organism lastingly extin- "guished by a* STRONGER ONE, *if this (differing from it in kind,) is very "similar to that in its manifestation.*"

(p. 95.) "§ 27. Hence, the healing power of the medicines RESTS "(§ 12—26) upon their symptoms similar to the disease AND *overpoising "the same in force*, thus every single case of disease being most surely, "radically, and speedily, and lastingly annihilated and abolished, only "by *that* medicine which is itself able to beget (in the human system), "the totality of the symptoms in the most similar and complete manner, "AND *which at the same time* EXCEEDS the disease *in force.*"

(p. 100.) "§ 34. The greater strength of the artificial diseases to be "produced by medicines, is, however, not the only condition for their "power of curing the natural diseases. Just above all, for the cure, it is "required, that they should be able to beget in the human body an arti- "ficial disease most possibly similar to the disease which is to be cured, "so as to put itself, *by their simility* COUPLED *with a somewhat greater "strength*, in the place of the natural disease-affection, and *in this way* to "deprive it of all impression upon the vital force."

(p. 122.) § 51. "To the able mind of man this Law" (heal by Symptom Simility, § 50) "is revealed by them [symptoms], and they were "sufficient for that purpose. But, behold! what an advantage has not "man above rude nature in its accidental occurrences! How many "thousands more of homœopathic morbific potencies does not man "everywhere possess in the medicinal substances which are spread all "over creation for the help to the suffering fellowmen? They are to him "parents of diseases of all possible effect—varieties, for all the innumer-"able, for all the thinkable and unthinkable natural diseases against "which they can furnish homœopathical help, morbific potencies [medi-"cinal substances], the strength of which, overcome by the vital force "after the completed curative application, disappears by itself, without "wanting any reiterated help for driving them away again, like the itch, "*artificial disease-potencies which the physician can rarefy, distribute,* "POTENTIATE, *and* LESSEN IN THEIR DOSE, TO SUCH A POINT, *that they* "*remain* ONLY *a* LITTLE STRONGER *than the similar natural disease to be* "*cured by them,* so that with this unsurpassable mode of healing, it needs "no violent attack upon the organism, to root out even an old and obsti-"nate evil; yea, that this mode of healing is merely seen in a gentle, "*imperceptible,* and yet often speedy transition from the torturing natural "sufferings to the lasting health desired."

(p. 133.) § 61 . . . . "They [the allœopathic physicians] would "have perceived that . . . . *the homœopathic application* of the medicines "according to their Symptom Simility must bring about a permanent, "complete cure, IF *with it* the *opposite of their large doses,* THE VERY "LEAST OF ALL, *be given.*

(p. 138.) § 68. "[These incontrovertible truths] show us in homœo-"pathic cures, that upon the *uncommonly little doses* which were *just only* "*sufficient,* by the simility of their symptoms, to overtune (ueberstimmen), "and to push away the similar natural disease, though, after the extir-"pation of the latter, at first some medicine-disease still continues in the "organism, yet, *because of the extraordinary littleness of the dose,* so "transient, so slight, and so soon disappearing by themselves, that the "vital force needs no more significant reaction against this little artificial "distemper [Verstimmung] of its state, than is requisite for raising the "present state to the healthy standpoint, that is, to the full restoration, "for which end little effort is wanted after the extinction of the preceding "morbid distemper.

(p. 187.) § 128. "The modern and most modern experiences have "taught—that the medicine-substances in their crude state, when taken "by the proving person for the purpose of proving their peculiar effects, "do not, by far, utter the full richness of the forces being latent in them, "as [they do] when, for that purpose they have been taken *in high rare-* "*factions* [hohen Verduennungen], potentiated by proper trituration and "succussion, by which simple operation the forces which lay hidden, and "as it were, dormant, in their crude condition, are incredibly developed "and awakened into activity."

"Thus, now, even the substances hitherto deemed to be weak, are "BEST searched into, regarding their medicinal virtues, by causing the "proof-person, daily, before meals, to take four to six *finest pellets with "the thirtieth potentiated attenuation of such a substance, moistened with a "little water*, and to continue the same several days."

(p. 188.) § 129. [In proving] "it is very advisable, to make the "beginning first with *a little dose* of medicine, and, where commensurate "and requisite, to ascend from day to day to *a higher and higher dose.*"

(p. 246.) § 230. [In cases of mental or emotional disease, when "the selected remedies are homœopathically commensurate] . . . "the "*least possible doses* often are *sufficient*, to produce the most striking "improvement in not very long time."

(p. 255.) § 242. "We, then, have to deal only with a psoric intermit-"tent fever, which usually is vanquished *by the finest doses of* Sulphur "and Hep. sul. calc. *in High Potency, rarely repeated.*

(p. 257.) § 246. "On the contrary, slowly progressing amelioration, "after *one dose of strikingly homœopathic* selection, IF IT IS VERY FINE, "indeed, also accomplishes sometimes, in its uninterruptedly continuing "duration of action, that help which this remedy, according to its nature, "is capable to effect in this case, in spaces of time of forty, fifty, one "hundred days. But, partly, this is rarely the case, partly it is of much "import as well to the physician as to the patient, that, if it were pos-"sible, this period could be shortened to one-half, to one-quarter, and "even more, and that in this manner a much speedier healing could be "gained. And THIS, too, can be very successfully carried out, as recent "and often repeated experiences have taught us, UNDER THE CONDITIONS: "First, if the medicine with all circumspection was selected very strik-"ingly homœopathical,—Second, IF *it is administered* IN THE FINEST DOSE "least revolting and yet duly attuning [umstimmenden] the vital force; "and, Thirdly, if such a *finest forceful dose* of the best selected medicine, "is repeated in commensurate spaces of time."

(p. 259.) Note 1. "LEAST, I say, since it stands, and will stand, *as a "homœopathic rule of cure*, refutable by no experience in the world, *that "of the rightly chosen remedy the* BEST DOSE IS ALWAYS THE LEAST ONE "IN ONE OF THE HIGH POTENTIATIONS (30), as well for chronic as for "acute diseases—a truth which is the invaluable *property of pure Homœo-"pathy*, which, as long as Allœopathy (and not much less the modern "mongrel-sect, composed of allœopathic and homœopathic treatment) "yet continues to gnaw, like a cancer, upon the life of the sick men, and "to corrupt them with greater and greatest doses of medicine, which will "keep remote from the pure Homœopathy these false arts by an un-"fathomable gulf."

(p. 269.) § 252. "In the *commensurate* (LEAST) *dose.*"

(p. 270.) § 253. Note 1. "The symptoms of amelioration in min "and spirit are to be expected soon after the taking of the medicine *only* "*then, when* THE DOSE *was* DULY (*i. e.* MOST POSSIBLY) LITTLE."

" . . . . Here I remark, that this so necessary rule, is mostly sinned "against by the presumptuous beginners in Homœopathics, and by the "physicians going out of the old school over to the Homœopathical "Healing Art. These, from old prejudices, abhor the LEAST DOSES of the "deepest rarefactions [tiefste verduennungen] of the medicines in such "cases, and they must lack the great advantages and blessings of that "treatment, which, in thousand experiences, has been found to be the "most wholesome, and *cannot accomplish* what true Homœopathics can, "and hence, unjustly palm themselves off as her disciples."

(p. 280.) § 269. "The Homœopathical Healing Art developes for its "purposes *the spirit-like medicine-force of the crude substances* by an ope-"ration *peculiar to it*, hitherto unattempted, *to a degree heretofore unheard* "*of*, by which they all become only right penetratingly efficacious and "helpful, even those, which, in raw condition, betray not the least medi-"cine-force in the human body."

(p. 284.) § 275. "*The commensurateness of a medicine* for a given case "of disease RESTS NOT ONLY upon its striking homœopathic selection, "but JUST AS WELL *upon the requisite correct magnitude* or RATHER "LITTLENESS OF ITS DOSE.

(p. 286.) § 278. "Here now arises the question, which is this degree "of littleness most commensurate for help partly certain, partly gentle; "HOW LITTLE, then, THE DOSE OF EVERY SINGLE REMEDY, *homœopathi-*"*cally selected* for a case of disease, *must be* for the purpose of the best "cure?"

"To solve this problem, and, for every medicine in particular to deter-"mine *which dose* of it is *sufficient* for the object of the *homœopathic* cure, "and which is *still so little*, as to accomplish by it the gentlest and "speediest cure, to solve this problem, is, as can easily be seen, *not the* "*work of theoretical guess, not by the speculative understanding, not by subtle* "*sophistry the solution of this problem is to be expected; solely pure experi-*"*ments, careful observation, and correct experience, can determine this, and* "*it would be foolish to adduce* the great doses of inadequate (allœopathic) "medicine of the old school-practice which do not homœopathically "touch the diseased side of the organism, but only attack the parts un-"attacked by the disease, against that, what *pure experience* pronounces "on THE NECESSARY LITTLENESS OF DOSE for the purpose of *homœopathic* "cures."

(p. 287.) § 279. "This *pure experience shows throughout*, that, if not "evidently a considerable corruption of some important viscera is at the "bottom of the disease, (even if belonging to the chronic and compli-"cated ones), and, if in the cure all other medicinal influences, from "without, upon the patient, have been kept away; *the dose of the homœo-*"*pathically selected remedy can never be prepared so little, as not to be still* "*stronger* than the natural disease, and as not to be capable, partly at "least, to overtune [ueberstimmen], extinguish, and heal it, so long, as it "(the dose) is still capable, immediately after taking, to cause its symp-"toms to be heightened somewhat, however little, above the disease "similar to it. (Slight homœopathic aggravation § 157–160.")

(p. 288.) § 280. "This incontrovertible, experiential position, is the "*measure, according to which the doses of homœopathic* medicine, WITHOUT "EXCEPTION, *have to be lessened* to such a point, that, after taking, they "excite only a hardly perceptible homœopathic aggravation, *the lessening "may descend ever so low, and appear ever so incredible to the grossly mate-"rial notions of the every-day-physicians.* Their talk must grow dumb "before the verdict of the infallible experience.

(p. 289.) § 281. "Every patient is, especially in point of his disease, "incredibly attunable [umstimmbar] by medicinal potencies, adequate by "Effect-Simility, and there is NO man, ever so robust, affected even with a "chronic or so-called local evil, who would not soon feel the most desired "change in the suffering part, when he has taken the helpful, *homœopathi-"cally commensurate medicine* IN THE LEAST CONCEIVABLE DOSE, in one "word, whose condition would not be THEREBY changed far more, than "the one day old, but healthy, suckling by the same.

"How insignificant, and ridiculous, therefore, is the merely *theoretical "unbelief*, against these never failing infallible evidences of experience."

(p. 291.) § 283. "Now, in order to proceed truly according to nature, "the *true healing artist will prescribe* his well selected *homœopathic* medi-"cine EXACTLY IN SO LITTLE A DOSE ONLY, as *is just even sufficient* to "overtune and annihilate the disease,—*in a littleness of dose*, by which, "if human frailty should once have misled him, to apply a less adequate "medicine, the injury done is lessened to insignificance, the disadvantage "of its quality being inadequate to the disease, which (disadvantage), "*from the* MOST POSSIBLY LEAST DOSE, is also much too weak, as not "forthwith to be extinguished and made good again, by the own force of "the nature of life, and by the prompt opposition of the remedy selected, "now in adequate Effect Simility."

(p. 293.) Note. . . . "And when there is reason for applying, to a "very sensitive patient, THE LEAST POSSIBLE DOSE, and to bring about "the speediest result; then the *mere smelling once* is serviceable."

(p. 295.) Note 1. "*The higher* the rarefaction connected with poten-"tiation (by two succussive strokes), is carried, *the speedier* and *the more "penetrative* appears, medicinally, the effect of the preparation, to give "another tune to the vital force, and to change the state, with but little "lessened strength, EVEN WHEN *this operation is carried* VERY FAR, in-"stead to 30, as usual (and mostly sufficient), NOW TO 60, 150, 300 AND "HIGHER."

No limit, then, to Potentiation, is fixed by Hahnemann.

(p. 300.) Note 1. "The LEAST *homœopathic dose* which, however, often "works wonders in the proper place. Not rarely the imperfect Homœo-"pathicians, deeming themselves *superfluously* wise, *overcharge* their "patients in severe diseases, *by doses* of different medicines, rapidly suc-"ceeding each other, *although* homœopathically selected and adminis-

"tered in highpotentiated rarefaction; and thus they place them [the "patients] in a state so over excited, that life and death are at war with "each other, etc."

In the years 1835 and 1839, the second and last edition of the "Chron. Krankheiten" was published. The following quotations will show, that Hahnemann went on, in the original and initial direction of the Infinitesimality of the Dose, and most decidedly and unmistakeably so.

1835. (Chron. Krankh., 2 ed., Dresd. & Lpzg, Arnold. vol. I, p. 149.) "Generally, the physician, next to the unhomœopathic selection of the "remedy, *cannot commit a greater fault*, than firstly, *of deeming* the doses "indicated in every antipsoric medicine and by me *moderated so far* after "manyfold experiments (necessitated by experience) *to be too little;* "secondly, the incorrect selection of the remedy; and thirdly, the pre-"cipitation, not to let it work sufficiently without interruption."

"Of the first *main fault* I have spoken just now, and I merely add, "that *nothing* is neglected IF *we administer the doses* (*if it were possible*) "STILL LESSER THAN I HAVE INDICATED MYSELF. ONE CANNOT, "ALMOST, GIVE THEM TOO LITTLE."

1837. (Chr. Krankh. vol. III., p. vi., note.) "In treating acute cases, "the homœopathic physician acts in a similar manner: He dissolves one "(two) globules of the *highpotentiated* well selected medicine in 7, 10, 15 "tablespoonfuls of water (without admixtion), by shaking of the bottle, "and lets the patient, according as the evil is more or less acute, more or "less dangerous, take one or one-half teaspoonful every half hour, or "two, three, four, five and six hours."

1838. (Chr. Krankh., vol. V., p. iv.) "Already, then, *in the fiftieth* "*Potency*, (the modern wise-acres, hitherto, would scoff at the thirtieth "potency already, and they had to content themselves with the low, "little-developed, more massive preparations of medicine in high doses, "by which, however, they could not accomplish what our Healing Art "can do)—we have got . . . . *medicines of the most penetrating effica-* "*ciousness.*"

Further on, in the years 1842 and 1843, we find a report of two cures by Hahnemann, published by Bœnninghausen in the "Neues Archiv für die Homœopathische Heilkunst Leipzig, Schumann, 1844," vol. I., 1, p. 79. These cures show most conclusively, that Hahnemann, almost to his very last breath, (he died in 1843, July 2d, 89 years of age), followed out the original and fundamental idea of Homœopathy—Infinitesimality,—which he had discovered and developed to growing perfection, in the course of a long and eventful life of conscientious labor for the welfare of mankind.

These prescriptions in the first of these cases were the following:

(p. 80.) 1842, Sept. 12. Insanity after sunstroke, in a girl fourteen years old. Bellad. lenified (gelinderte) Dynamization (according to Bœnninghausen, one globule of the sixtieth Potency) dissolved in seven teaspoonfuls of water; of this solution one-tablespoonful dissolved in one glass of water (about the size of a tumbler), and, after stirring, one teaspoonful of this latter solution was to be taken in the morning.

Sept. 16, the fifth day after, the following dose was ordered : one-teaspoonful of the last mentioned solution, to be stirred into a second tumbler of water, and two to four teaspoonfuls (daily increasing by one), to be taken in the morning.

Sept. 20, the fifth day after, one globule of Bellad., Higher Potency, dissolved in seven-tablespoonfuls of water, one-tablespoonful to be mixed in a tumbler of water, and one-teaspoonful to be taken every morning for six days.

Sept. 28, the ninth day after, Hyosc. $\frac{1}{30}$ in seven-tablespoonfuls of water, one-tablespoonful mixed in a tumbler of water, and one-teaspoonful to be taken in the morning.

Oct. 5, the eighth day after, Sacch. lact., prepared and given in similar manner.

Oct. 18, the fourteenth day after Sulph. (*new Dynamization of the least substance*) one globule, potentiated through three tumblers, one-teaspoonful in the morning.

Oct. 22, the fifth day after, Sulph., *next Dynamization*, *potentiated* through two tumblers.

This was used with interruption till November, when the patient was well.

The other case was that of a man thirty-three years old. Syphilitic sore throat and Hæmorrhoids. The prescriptions were as follows :

1843, Jan. 15. Bell. *thirty of the then lowest Dynamization*, dissolved in seven tablespoonfuls of water, of which one tablespoonful was well mixed in a tumbler full of water, one teaspoonful in the morning after rising.

Jan. 18. Merc. v. one globule of the lowest *new Dynamization* (*which contains much less substance than the one hitherto made*), prepared and taken in the same way.

Jan. 20. Merc. v. ($\frac{2}{0}$) of the second of such Dynamizations, prepared in the same way, and taken in the morning.

Jan. 30. Sacch lact., prepared and taken the same.

Feb. 7. Sulph. $\frac{2}{0}$ as above.

Feb. 13. Gave him a smelling dose of Merc. and Merc. v. $\frac{II}{0}$, one globule as above.

Feb. 20. Sacch. lact. as above.

March 3. Nitri ac. by olfaction, and Sacch. lact. as above.

March 20. Nitri ac. by olfaction, by opening a small vial containing half an ounce of ordinary spirit of wine or brandy, in which one globule of medicine is dissolved, and smelling for one or two moments. Patient was then well.

Finally we have the evidence given by Croserio, in a letter to Bœnninghausen, dated January 28, 1844, and published in the Neues Archiv, Vol. I., 2, p. 30. Croserio was, of the Parisian Homœopathicians, the one most intimate with Hahnemann, visited him almost daily, and thus had the best opportunity of knowing, how Hahnemann prescribed in his latter days. The following passages are to the purpose.

"Hahnemann always used only the well-known little globules, com-"monly moistened with the thirtieth dilution, as well for acute as for "chronic cases. Of these globules he had one, or at most two, dissolved "and well shaken in a caraffe, containing fifteen tablespoonfuls of water "and one-half or a whole tablespoonful of (French) brandy. *Only one* "*tablespoonful of the solution* was put in a tumbler of water, and *of* "*this last* the patient took *only by teaspoonfuls*, that is to say, on the first "day one teaspoonful, on the second two, on the third three, and so on, "daily one teaspoonful more, until he noticed effect. He then *lessened* "*the dose*, or ordered to cease taking medicine entirely. In other cases "he ordered a teaspoonful of the first tumbler to be poured into a second "tumbler of water, in others again, from this second a spoonful into a "third, and so on to a sixth tumbler, *only one teaspoonful to be taken* "*from the last tumbler, when he had to deal with very excitable persons.* "Only in rare cases he allowed a table or teaspoonful of the first solution "in 8–15 tablespoonfuls of water, to be taken once a day . . . . . In the "last years of his practice Hahnemann appears to have applied his whole "dexterity to *lessening the doses more and more.* Hence in the last years "he made a very frequent use of *olfaction.* For this purpose he put one or "two globules in a small vial, containing two drachms of alcohol, diluted "with an equal quantity of water, and let them *smell only once or twice* "*by each nostril*, NEVER OFTENER. In this way my own wife was cured "by him, of a violent pleurisy, within five hours. In chronic diseases, "happen what might, he *never let them smell oftener than once a week*, "and give *nothing besides* for internal use, except mere sugar of milk, "and *in this manner* he effected the *most admirable cures*, even in such "cases *where all others had been unable to accomplish anything* . . . . "I can give you the assurance, he was most fully convinced that in *no* "*case it is necessary*, even not of use, to give the medicine in drops, and "that, from day to day more, *he satisfied himself of the noxiousness of* "LARGER *doses.*"

The facts speak for themselves. Anybody who desires still more facts, can find them in numerous other passages of the works of Hahnemann, besides those here presented. They all establish our position.

They prove, as a matter of history, that the Minimal Dose, the Infinitesimal Dose, belongs to Homœopathy, as originally and properly as the Simility of Symptoms.

They prove as a fact, that the founder of Homœopathy founded it equally on both the Infinitesimality and the Symptom Simility.

They prove, that he, from the very inception, established, and over and over again confirmed, the fact, and the rule based upon it, that the Least Dose of a Simile, a Minimum of it, is sufficient to effect the cure; and that he lessened the dose from little to less, from less to least, constantly on the same principle.

They prove, that both, the quantitative and qualitative elements, in natural and inseparable union, form the original and innate character of the Homœopathic Remedy, and so much so, that such remedy is impossible to be homœopathical, if not a Minimum and Simile at the same time.

They prove, that this peculiar quantitative character of Homœopathy, its Posology, is the very nature and criterion of it, distinguishing it from all other arts and manners of healing whatever.

They prove, that the principle of Infinitesimality is historically, from first to last, the leading idea of Homœopathic Posology.

They prove, historically, that *the infinitesimal dose is homœopathic.* And that being true, it is, in the converse, equally true, that the *homœopathic dose is infinitesimal!*

To conclude: Infinitesimality is, in verity, as fundamental, and as essential to Homœopathy, as Simility is. Both are equally inherent and proper to Homœopathy, and both have been so from the beginning throughout. This is a fixed fact, a historical fact, incontestable, and unalterable by afterthoughts, theories, trimmings, and criticisms.

The consequences are irresistible. No pretended Homœopathy can hold its ground against true Homœopathy. Development may modify; but a changeling has no legitimate title. Systems may be built and rebuilt; but the foundation remains the same. Opinions may differ; but they cannot alter the nature of the thing. Sophisms may shine; but they cannot unsettle the fact. Secession may try; but the Union must be preserved.

Previous to Hahnemann nobody had ever found, thought, or practised, the fundamental Law of Homœopathy, covering both the quantification and the qualification of the remedy. Hippocrates never thought of Potentiation. The Galenic school always cared and sought for the limit of the *Maximum* Dose. The new medicine, directly opposite, cares and seeks for the limit of the *Minimum* Dose. This is Hahnemann's work. Hahnemannian Homœopathy is the only Homœopathy known to History. After him, others may attempt to change, trim, appropriate, or falsify, the results of his labor, but the truth of history must prevail. It was Hahnemann, who established it as a fact, that the homœopathic remedy, a Simplex, to be curative, must be a Simile and Minimum at the same time. He it was, too, who for that purpose invented Potentiation, as the practical mode and method of lessening the quantity of medicine, so as to make it as fine as possible, and to obtain the proper remedial quantity, the minimal or infinitesimal dose.

Now, to cure by the Least Dose of a Simplex according to Symptom-Simility, this is the Homœopathic Law of Cure, and the whole of it. In its entirety it forms the very basis and nature of Homœopathy. The Principle of the Dose is contained in it.

This principle is the postulate of common sense, that enough is sufficient, and here as much as necessary; that no more, and no greater quantity of medicine, is required for the cure, than there is just sufficient to change disease into health; and that, therefore, the least quantity of medicine, or an infinitesimal dose of it, if a Simile, is sufficient, and all that is required, for the cure.

Scientifically speaking, the Least Plus, *ceteris paribus*, is sufficient for the change; and, since the Least Plus is infinitesimal by nature, the infinitesimal must necessarily be sufficient; and, since here the sufficient dose is all that is necessary, it follows, that the infinitesimal dose is all that is necessary for the cure.

The practical question in the given case, how much of the homœopathic remedy is sufficient for the cure, resolves itself into the question: how little is necessary? This is determined by experiment. History shows, that experience, gradually, proved less and less to be sufficient. From our own experience we are satisfied, that a Homœopathic Potency as high as one hundred thousand, centesimally, is a quantity still great enough, and not too little, to be efficacious.

When we can accomplish the purpose by a little infinitesimal dose, why should we try to do it by large or massive administrations, taxing the system more than is required for the purpose?

Better no medicine, than too much of it! But better the least infinitesimal dose of a homœopathic medicine, than no medicine at all! Strictly following Hahnemann in the preparation and dose, as well as in the selection of the remedy, and thus only, we shall be able to uphold Homœopathy in its integrity, and to fulfil the higher ethical duties of the conscientious physician as a true friend of mankind.

Whoever recognizes the Homœopathic Law of Cure, and acts upon it in his profession, professes Homœopathy and is a Homœopathician. Whoever professes Homœopathy, is, by his own act, concluded against disputing its Law, or breaking it, or repudiating any essential part of it.

Such an essential part is the Law of the Dose, contained in its Law of the Cure. The Homœopathic Posology is, and always has been, a constituent and integral part of Homœopathy; and, in fact, it is its diacritical element.

Is it, then, admissible or excusable in any man, professing Homœopathy, to accept its Materia Medica alone without its Posology? Is it sense for any man, who owns a thing, to throw off one half of it, and at the same time to claim, that he keeps the whole of it?

And yet, this is precisely what many of our brethren, in Europe and in this country, are attempting to do. *Charity* compels us to believe it to be a sad honest mistake. But it is a strange infatuation indeed! If persisted in, through misplaced *Liberty*, it destroys the innate *Unity* of Homœopathy. Leading to a Sectarianism or Schism, as wanton as disgraceful, it would much impede our progress, because opening the door to a spirit of exclusivity and proscription. The end of it may be, perhaps, that the bisecting and dimorphous half-homœopathicians fraternize, and by and by coalesce, with the half-allœopathicians, and that both together subside in the space gradually yielded up by the improvements going on in the allœopathic school, and perchance, by degrees, form a beautiful new compound, unknown to fame and without a name as yet, but clearly not entitled to the name or estate of Homœopathy.

However, *magna est veritas, et prævalebit!*

APPENDIX.

II.

GEOMETRICAL ILLUSTRATIONS

OF THE

HOMŒOPATHIC REMEDIAL PROCESS,

PROBATIVE AND CURATIVE.

Les semblables se guerissent des semblables

DES CARTES.

Man kann es mit der Diagonale zweier Kræfte vergleichen.

HERING.

ACCORDING to the Observations 21 and 22 in the Fourth Series:—"The Laws of Motion serve as the mathematical principle of Homœopathy;" and "Under these laws the homœopathic remedial process, probative and curative, is geometrically demonstrable, being, as Hering observes, comparable to the diagonal of two forces, and the parallelogram of forces is *its geometrical* illustration."*

I.

The organism is a material point, formed, preserved, and propelled in the Universe, on our planet, by a system of cosmological and biological motions or forces, representing motions, according to the Laws of Motion, formulized by Newton, as follows:

"*Lex I.* Corpus omne perseverare in statu quo suo quiescendi vel movendi uniformiter in directum, nisi quatenus a viribus impressis cogitur statum illum mutare.

"*Lex II.* Mutationum motus proportionalem esse vi motrici impressæ et fieri secundum lineam rectam, qua vis illa imprimitur.

"*Lex III.* Actioni contrariam semper et æqualem esse reactionem; sive corporum duorum actiones in se mutuo semper esse æquales et in partes contrarias dirigi." (Principia. London, 1687, p. 12.)

Thus the organism presents in its healthy condition a system of uniform biological motions, in a normal state of oscillating equilibrium, which is the equalization of all the physical and tension-forces, or, what Draper well designates as the mechanical and chemical equilibrium of the system of man.

---

* See page 47, ante.

II.

(1.) The biological system of motions which is the healthy state of the organism, may be represented, by the sum of these motions in oscillating equilibrio, as a force impressed in a rectilinear direction upon a point representing the organism, which is the resultant or diagonal of the parallelograms of all the forces, constituting this equilibrium, and it may, as such, be projected in a perpendicular line, A B, (Fig. 1,) let fall upon the plane of existence X.

Fig. 1.

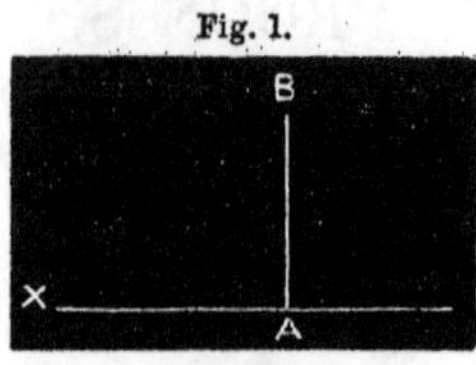

This direction we will call the *biotic* line.

Fig. 2.

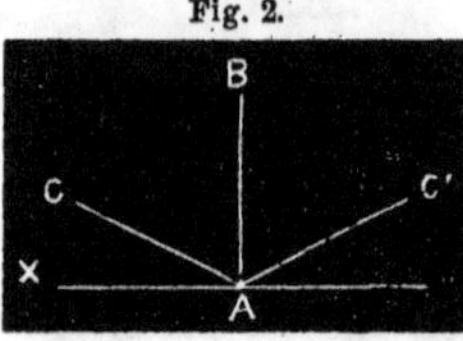

(2.) Any force or agent, whatever it be aetiologically, may cause a change of the direction of the biotic line, by acting upon it, on either side, at any angle, thus causing an alteration of this direction.

This we will call a *pathematic* line or force or potency, A C, A C', (Fig. 2.)

Fig. 3

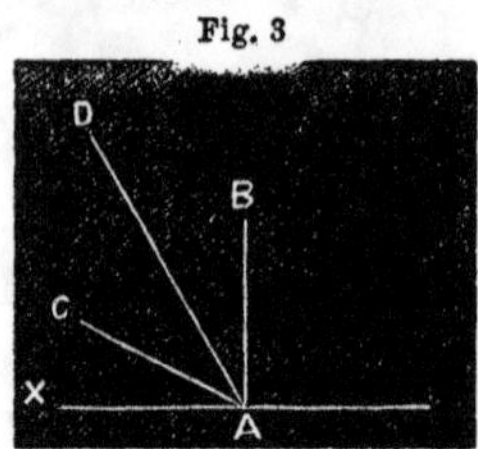

(3.) If a force or potency, A C, (Fig. 3,) be impressed and act upon one side of the biotic line in a given angle, the direction of the biotic will change in the direction of the resultant of the potency and of the biotic, A D.

This represents the perturbation of health of the organism, and we will call this force or potency the *pathopoetic* force or potency.

Fig. 4.

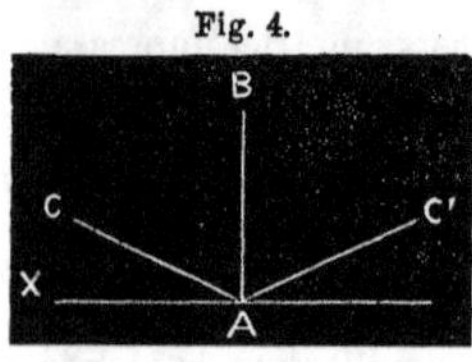

(4.) If another equal force or potency A C' (Fig. 4,) be impressed, and act, opposite and on the contrary side to the biotic line, and at the same angle with the pathopoetic, and at the same instant, then the original direction of the biotic line, A B, will be sustained or immediately restored.

This represents the restoration of health in a prototype, and we will, therefore, call this force or potency *hygiopoetic.*

(5.) If the resultant of the pathopoesis, (Fig. 3,) after it has lasted without any counteraction a given time, be represented by A D,

Fig. 5.

(Fig. 5,) and if a hygiopoetic force be applied in the same angle in which the pathopoetic force A C was impressed, on the contrary side, then these two forces or potencies, being equal and opposed, will neutralize each other, and enable the changed biotic to resume its normal healthy action A F, as shown in the parallel A B, (Fig. 3,) and A F, (Fig. 5.)

This represents the restoration of health, by a potency, after the disease has lasted a given time, and illustrates the *homœopathic curative process proper*.

Fig. 6.

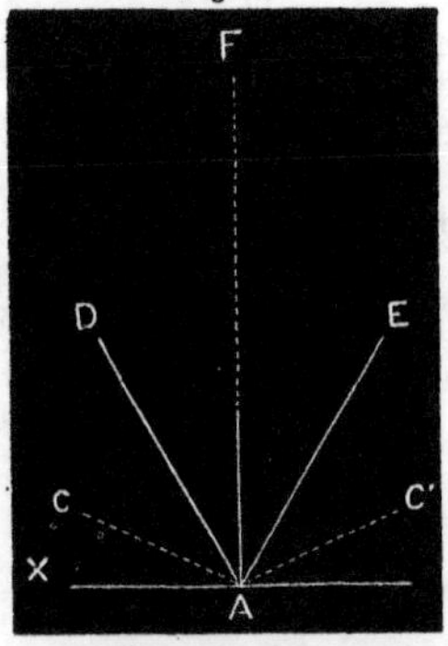

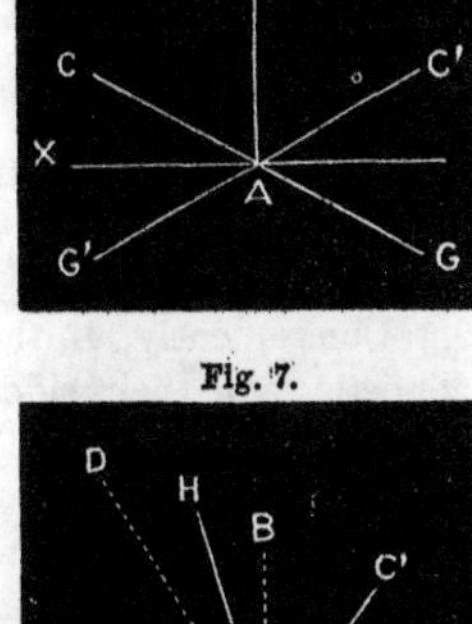

(6.) If the pathopoetic force A C be such as to act upon the organism with an intensity exceeding the biological forces by their own amount, and more, then the organism will, under the preponderating power, be carried, entirely in the direction of the pathopoetic force, out of the plane of its existence A G, A G′, (Fig. 6.)

This would represent *death* by accident, poisons, lightning, suffocation, etc.

Fig. 7.

(7.) If the organism be exposed to the action of the pathopoetic force A C, (Fig. 7,) for a length of time, and then it should be acted upon by another pathopoetic force, A C′, in the shape of a remedy, at an angle different from that of the pathopoetic with the biotic, then the result will be another oblique line, A H.

This would represent the *allœopathic* method of treating disease.

Fig. 8.

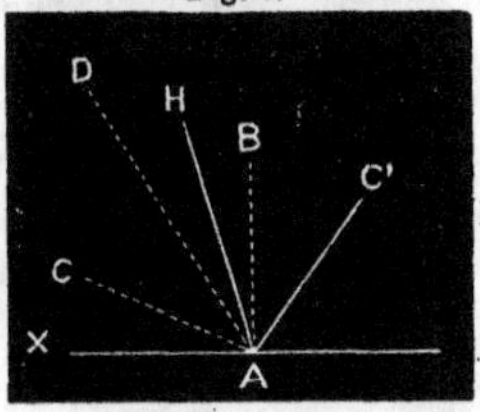

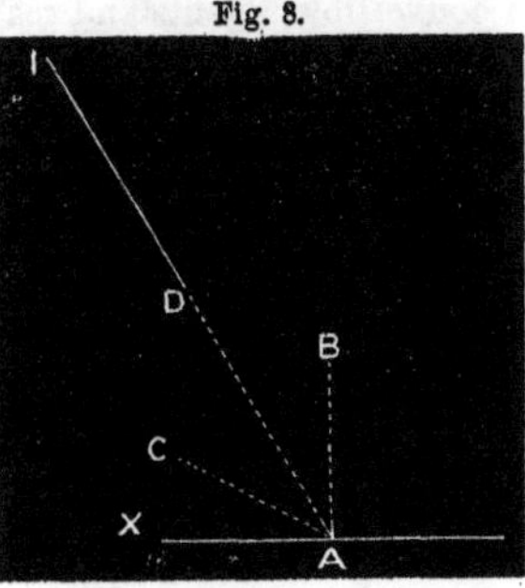

(8.) If the organism be impressed by a pathopoetic force, A C, (Fig. 8,) and if another pathopoetic force, A I, of the same magnitude, be opposed diametrically to the resultant oblique line; then the latter will be neither changed nor restored, but remain in statu quo as long as the forces be equal, and move in the direction of the greater one, if the one preponderates over the other.

This would represent the *enantiopathic* method of treating disease.

Fig. 9.

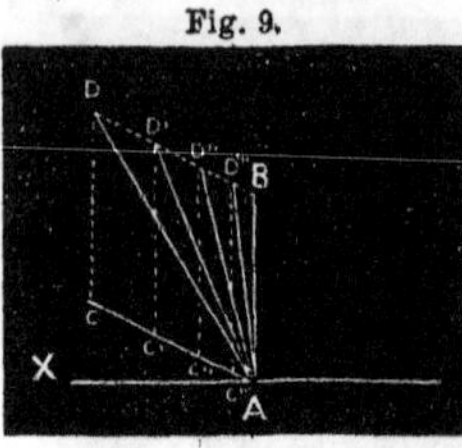

(9.) If the pathopoetic action A C, (Fig. 9,) decrease A C′, A C″, A C‴, under the co-operation of the biological forces A B, by the assimilation and neutralization of the same, then, by virtue of its self-preservation, sustained by the biological forces, the organism will tend to resume, and finally actually regain, the perpendicular normal biotic line A B, by imperceptible degrees.

This would represent the process of *spontaneous recovery*.

III.

(1.) It makes no difference, whether the potency impressed on either side of the biotic line A B, (Fig. 2,) be impressed by nature, accident, poison, drug, experimentally, or otherwise. The potency will, in either case, be pathopoetic (as in the probative process) or hygiopoetic, (as in the curative process,) and the difference is only in the application of the one or the other to the one or the other contrary side of the biotic line.

(2.) Consequently, if the two forces or potencies, pathopoetic and hygiopoetic, and their sides of application, were exchanged, the result would be exactly the same, in the converse, as above described.

(3.) Hence the same force or potency is neither pathopoetic nor hygiopoetic PER SE, but it becomes either the one or the other only by relation, that is to say, according as it is applied to one side of the biotic line, (*e. g.* to the healthy organism as proving,) or to the contrary side, (*e. g.* to the diseased organism as remedy,) and *vice versa*.

(4.) Hence the said pathematic forces are equivalent, interchangeable, and convertible, agents and reagents, making and unmaking the disease, as the case may be.

(5.) *Now*, the very property and nature of a substance which is known as a homœopathic potency, is this, that, if applied to the healthy, it acts pathematically: causing the symptoms of the disease which are similar to those which appear in the diseased organism as the disease, in the given case, (Fig. 3.)

(6.) Therefore, the same homœopathic potency, if applied to the diseased organism, must, naturally and necessarily, act pathematically again: causing a removal of the symptoms of disease which are similar to those which appear by its application to the healthy organism as disease, in the given case, or causing the production of the symptoms of health which are similar to those which appear in the healthy organism as health, in the given case, (Fig. 5.)

(7.) And, *therefore*, the homœopathic potency is homœopathical and homœodynamical, pathopoetic and hygiopoetic, making and unmaking the disease, as the case may be.

Q. E. D.

IV.

Fig. 10.

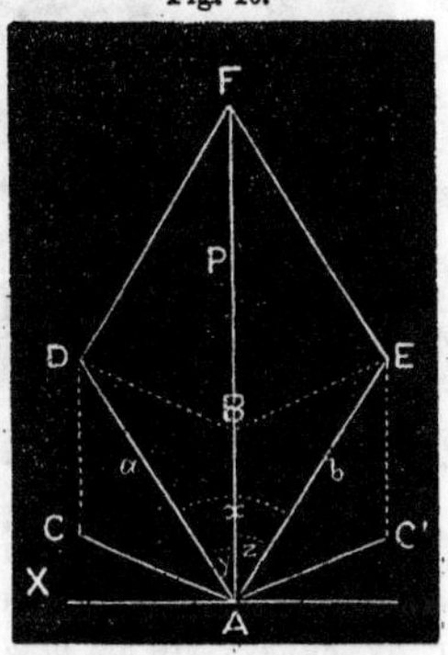

(1.) The parallelogram of the pathopoetic and hygiopoetic forces drawn out, exhibits and illustrates, in each given case, (Fig. 10.)

Mutual Action,

Simility,

Contrariety, and

Infinitesimality.

(2.) The *Mutual Action* is, that either force, A C and A C′, is impressed, and acts together with the other, upon the same organism, and that the same organism is affected by both at the common point A, (Fig. 5.)

(3.) The *Simility* is in the equality of the angles *y* and *z* of the pathopoesis A D and hygiopoesis A E, (Fig. 10); in the equality of the angles of the pathopoetic and hygiopoetic lines C A B, C′A B; in the parallelism of the restored perpendicularity of the biotic A F with the original one A B; in the equality of the pathopoetic parallelogram A B D C with the hygiopoetic A B E C′; and in the simility of the pathopoetic and hygiopoetic parallelograms to the parallelogram of the conjoint Mutual Action of the biotic pathopoetic and hygiopoetic forces A B D C and A B E C′ ∾ A D F E.

The reason, why these parallelograms are always unequal, though similar, lies in the susceptibility of the diseased organism for the hygiopoetic force.

This susceptibility varies in proportion to the assimilability of the remedy by the organism. When the assimilability of the remedy is greater, then the susceptibility of the organism is higher; and *vice versa*, the susceptibility of the organism is lower, when the assimilability of the remedy is lesser. This depends upon the degree of Simility of the pathopoetic pictures, (derived from natural and experimental disease,) and upon the potentiality (Leistungsfaehigkeit) of the organism.

The varying therapeutical relation, or Proportionality between Susceptibility and Assimilability of organism and remedy, is expressed by having the resultant E of the hygiopoesis lengthened, (Fig. 11,) or shortened, (Fig. 12,) as the case may be.

Fig. 11.

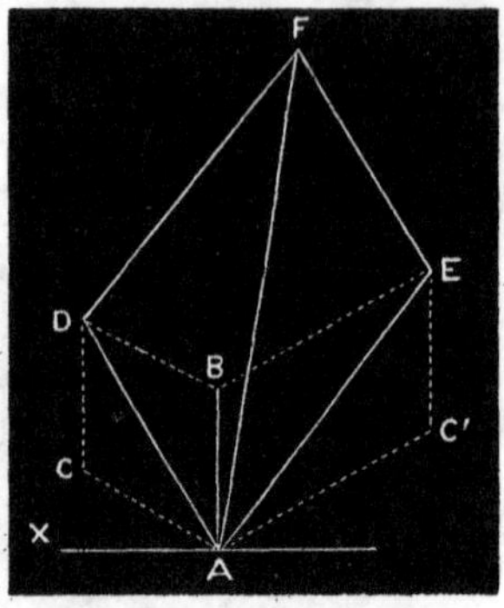

Fig. 12.

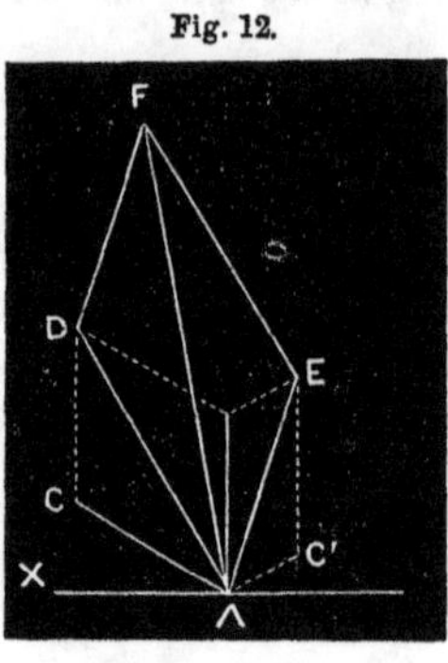

For, the line of the changed biotic force is already, by composition of the biotic with the pathopoetic force, larger than the original one. Hence the hygiopoesis, to be effective in overcoming the pathopoesis, must be proportioned to that quantity, which is represented by the changed biotic force, (Fig. 10.)

From this apportionment, then, necessarily, results the Simility of the two parallelograms, pathopoetic and hygiopoetic, with the parallelogram of the conjoint Mutual Action of all the forces concerned.

(4.) The *Contrariety* is, that the two forces are impressed, and act, in opposition, and on contrary sides, to the organism, and to each other.

(5.) The *Infinitesimality* is shown in the gradual neutralization of the pathopoetic and hygiopoetic forces, and in the least possible quantity of action, effecting the change, and represented in the cure by Homœopathic High Potencies.

This is demonstrable by the following train of reasoning:

If the biotic force A B, (Fig. 5,) and the pathopoetic force A C, solicit the organism in A with equal and invariable velocity, then these forces will continually and gradually neutralize each other, acting upon the organism in the direction of the resultant A F.

This proceeds, under Leibnitz's *Law of Continuity*, by infinite, successive, infinitesimal equalizations of the Mutual Action of the said forces, acting upon the organism.

Thus the hygiopoetic force, if applied at an equal angle with the pathopoetic force, vanishes together with the latter in the restored normal oscillating equilibrium of the biological forces, growing "smaller by degrees and beautifully less," as pointed out sub. II., under the head of spontaneous recovery.

If, according to a trigonometrical proposition applied to Mechanics, (Fig. 10,) $AF = p = \sqrt{(a^2 + b^2 + 2ab \cos. \Phi)}$, as the resultant of the biotic, pathopoetic and hygiopoetic forces in a given time, then the resistance or reaction of the organism R to these forces will be $R = p - \sqrt{(a^2 + b^2 + 2ab \cos. \Phi)} = 0$, that is to say, the Mutual Action of the biotic, and pathopoetic and hygiopoetic forces is the least possible quantity of action required to effect the change in the given case, and, therefore, the organism then will be in oscillating equilibrio, composed of all the biological motions, which constitute the human organism.

On the strength of the Equality of action and reaction alone, it is not conceivable, by Newton's Laws of Motion, how a body could move at all. But we deduce from Maupertuis' demonstration of the Least Quantity of Action, that *action and reaction themselves are effected by the* LEAST PLUS (*increment*) *being added to the mutual action on either the positive or the negative side.*

This *Least Plus*, the PLUS PER SE, is, essentially, an infinitesimal quantity, and is always the *Minimum* of the given action.

Hence, when action takes place, the equilibrium of the moving body must be disturbed by some force, and that, on close examination, appears to be only the last term of an infinite increasing series of prior actions and reactions, or equalizations of mutual actions.

Thus it is, that no equilibrium ever presents itself in reality, but what presents itself at the moment of observation, is, actually, the *Least Plus*, which runs, eternally, in a perpetual flux, through all things, mediating the motion of all things, large and small.

The equation of action and reaction is, in strictness, only a psychological fact, an abstraction, furnishing the means for assigning to the flowing quantities (Newton's Fluxions) a calculable limit which, in reality, nowhere exists.

To illustrate:

Denoting the series of Mutual Actions which make up the motion of a given body, furnishing the moving force or the motor, by a, and the Least Plus by α, and the body moved in consequence of the motion of a, by b, and supposing a and b to be equal or in equilibrio after the motion, it is proposed, that b would not have moved, as a consequence of the action and reaction of a and b, if α had been wanting in this Mutual Action of a and b; for $a + \alpha < b$ before the motion, and therefore,

$a + \alpha = b$.,...... ....I.)

Remark.—It does not matter, whether we take a to be an impelling mass, or a force of equal magnitude; for, whilst the shock is given to b, the shocking mass certainly constitutes the whole force acting upon b.

Here the motion of b would cease. If now, in infinitesimal time, another α will be added to it, the mutual action of a and b, which constitutes the motion of b, continues as long as α lasts;

$a+2\alpha=a_2$ ....II.)

And so on, if the motion of b is to continue, successive innumerable α's will have to be added, which, in an infinite series, give the finite motion, amenable to mathematical computation;

$a+n\alpha=b_n$ ....III.)

The mathematical details, calculations, and proofs, for this, belong to the province of Analytical Medics. Here it is sufficient to state, that O, which is commonly understood to be equivalent to nothing, is, in fact, not nothing, but an unassignable quantity, that is, virtually, the least assignable quantity. Taking the formula of the Resultant of two component forces acting upon a material point, for an example; $R=p-\sqrt{(a^2+b^2+ab \cos.\Phi)}=0$ does not imply nothing, but implies an equalization, of innumerable forces, for an infinitesimal element of time, plus the least quantity necessary, to keep up the action for the following equalization, in another infinitesimal of time, and so on. This notation, O, contains and covers, in fact, our infinitesimal Plus, which is the intermedium of all motion.

The curative action of a *Homœopathic High Potency* is, actually, such an *Infinitesimal Plus*, being a least possible quantity added to the motions and actions of the given organism, and producing a change of the same.

Thus, a Homœopathic High Potency, being analytically an *Intermedium*, and practically a *Remedium*, is always efficacious as an *Infinitesimal.*

(6.) Now, *Mutuality*, (supra ad 2); *Simility*, (supra ad 3); *Contrariety*, (supra ad 4); and *Infinitesimality*, (supra ad 5), are the very essential and constituent elements of the Mutual Action, which constitutes the homœopathic process, probative and curative. (See *Observ. Ser. III.*, 9, 31, 42, 73.)

(7.) AND the same are represented by the parallelograms of forces, as herein above drawn and explained.

(8.) THEREFORE, the parallelogram of forces is a geometrical illustration of the Homœopathic Remedial process, probative and curative.

Q. E. D.

NOTE.

The parallelogram of forces has never been satisfactorily explained. We are inclined to believe, that a better result would be obtained, if the physiological views, based upon Homœosis or Universal Assimilation, which are presented in our Observations, be accepted.

The material point which is acted on by the component forces, has always been considered as a mathematical point, because the mass of a body may be supposed to be concentrated at its centre of gravity. In consequence the materiality of this point has been altogether lost sight of. If two or more forces act upon a body at an angle, the body, by its constitution as a resistant body, reacts upon the forces in the same way, as the forces act upon him, viz. : by Mutual Action. Hence results a series of Mutual Actions, or equalizations of actions, which, being mediated by the Least Plus, move the body in the diagonal line. This resultant is, therefore, the equivalent of the Mutual Action between the body and the component forces, standing in the relation of assimilables and assimilatives.

Hitherto Science considers the body mostly with regard to its Inertia, as simply overcome by the forces. But this is a barren idea, incompatible with the reality and with the third Newtonian Law. Inertia is a negative conception. It is simply a negation of force and motion. Hence, by Inertia to account for motion, and for force as the cause of motion, is as illogical, and impracticable, as it is, to create something out of nothing. *Ex nihilo nihil fit.* Kepler's coupling "*vis*" with "*inertia*" does not help matters much. For "*vis inertiæ,*" if not a mere figure of speech, is a contradiction in terms.

Homœopathic Physiology seems to be destined to furnish a truer explanation of the principle of the parallelogram of forces.

Every component force may be analyzed and decomposed into infinitely many infinitesimal forces, acting simultaneously and continually. The same may be done with the action of any single force upon any body.

Force, strictly speaking, has only a psychological reality, being a mere abstraction, a logical term, to signify the resultant of a series of equalizations of actions and reactions, or of Mutual Actions, of bodies, mediated by the Least Plus. Hence we may consider force as opposite to, and contradistinguished from, the body acted on by it. Thus considered, force may be equal to the body, if the action of the force ceases after application, or it may be greater than the body acted on, if the motion, imparted to it by the force, continues. For, with the same right with which we, above, took the component force to be composed of infinitely many infinitesimal forces acting simultaneously and continually; we may, also, consider the body to be composed of infinitely many infinitesimal particles, so little in magnitude as to equal the infinitesimal particles of force, and endowed with corresponding acting forces, constituting the body, as the resultant of a series of equalizations of actions and reactions, or Mutual Actions, of forces, mediated by the Least Plus. Just so, the equilibrium is the result of the destruction of many forces which reciprocally combat and destroy the actions which they mutually exercise upon each other, (Lagrange.) In this view, force and body appear to be convertible terms, and like quantities, acting on each other*, and their comparison and calculation clearly fall within the dominion of Mathematics.

* See article "Potencies," in the Hahnemannian Monthly, Vol. I., p. 59.

CIRCULAR.

At the request of a number of prominent physicians, who have had the opportunity of testing the High Potencies of Dr. B. FINCKE of Brooklyn, I have arranged to make them accessible to the profession generally. Dr. FINCKE has now consented to give over to the trade a number of his preparations, complete lists of which will be sent free by mail on application. Published reports of important cases, cured by these potencies, are already before the public, and all of them have been verified in practice.

Being appointed Sole Agent for Dr. B. FINCKE'S HIGH POTENCIES, I am prepared to fill orders.

The remedies will be put up in vials containing about 1000 pellets, closed and signed by the makers' own hand.

The price is $1 for the 1000th potency, and ten cents more for each additional thousand. Thus—

Lachesis,	1000	per Vial,	@	......................$1 00
"	6000	"	"	.... 1 50
"	11000	"	"	.... 2 00
"	16000	"	"	.... 2 50
"	21000	"	"	.... 3 00
"	41000	"	"	.... 5 00
"	71000	"	"	.... 8 00
Lachnantes t.	76000	"	"	.... 8 50

TERMS: INVARIABLY CASH IN ADVANCE.

Philadelphia, October, 1865.

A. J. TAFEL,
HOMŒOPATHIC PHARMACY,
No. 48 *North Ninth Street.*

www.ingramcontent.com/pod-product-compliance
Lightning Source LLC
LaVergne TN
LVHW021417110826
845150LV00007B/1965

* 9 7 8 1 4 2 5 5 1 0 1 5 2 *